CONTENTS

Introduction 1

PART ONE: THE PERSON OF THE HOLY SPIRIT

1. A Deeper Dimension 9

2. The Holy Spirit 23

3. The Father and the Holy Spirit 27

4. Jesus Christ the Son and the Holy Spirit 35

5. The Holy Spirit and You 41

PART TWO: THE WORK OF THE HOLY SPIRIT

6. The Work of the Holy Spirit 61

7. Deeper with the Precious Holy Spirit 85

8. A Mighty Rushing Wind 95

A Final Note 111

Notes 115

GOING
DEEPER
with the
HOLY
SPIRIT

BENNY HINN

Clarion Call Marketing

GOING DEEPER WITH THE HOLY SPIRIT
Published by
Clarion Call Marketing, Inc.
P.O. Box 610010
Dallas, Texas 75261

www.BennyHinn.org

ISBN: 1-59574-037-6

Printed in the United States of America

10 9 8 7 6 5 4 3 2 1

INTRODUCTION

A friend once told me an unforgettable story about his great-grandparents. For years they eked out a living on a farm in Kentucky then finally gave up and moved to Oklahoma because they heard it was the land of opportunity. The farm they'd sold and left behind in the Bluegrass State had been unproductive.

The new owner of the land discovered oil and became incredibly wealthy. Ironically, the reason the land hadn't produced for the previous owner was that it was so saturated with petroleum that nothing would grow.

Think of it! For years those dear people lived in poverty while beneath their feet lay all they needed. If they had understood anything about petroleum engineering or could have somehow found out about the resources nestled below the surface of the hard-rock soil, they could have tapped into these rich oil deposits and enjoyed financial success beyond their wildest dreams! Instead, they moved farther west and continued living in poverty and lack.

In much the same way we have the great resources of the Holy Spirit available, yet too many believers live on the surface, experiencing only spiritual poverty and frustration, not tapping into the spiritual riches just below the surface. We simply need to go deeper. The Holy Spirit stands ready to provide guidance, strength, and energy to carry out His plans: *"But ye shall receive power, after that the Holy Ghost is come upon you"* (Acts 1:8).

Deeper with the Holy Spirit

We need to recognize that the Holy Spirit is much more than a representative of God, the Supreme Being. He is the Spirit of the Yahweh we worship, the Spirit of I AM, the Spirit of the Lord of heaven and earth. This title for the Holy Spirit, the Spirit of the Lord, is used repeatedly in both the Old and New Testaments.

I challenge you to go deeper with the Spirit of God. I encourage you to make sure you are enjoying the deepest possible level of freedom and abundance by the Holy Spirit. If you are not, all you need to do is ask. He is your Helper, and He longs to unleash blessings upon you and your family.

A fresh anointing of the Holy Spirit will change your life and impact others through your walk with the Lord. As a result, you will be consumed by your longing to be used of God and to know His presence in a greater dimension than ever before.

The Holy Spirit wants to anoint you with His power, to give you victory over temptation, to instruct you in God's Word, to fill you with wisdom and revelation, and to equip you for ministry. Above all, He longs to have fellowship with you and to bring you into the presence of God Almighty.

And it is the Holy Spirit who makes the Father and His Son, the Lord Jesus, so real in our hearts and lives. That is why the apostle Paul earnestly desired for all believers to experience *"the fellowship of the Holy Spirit"* (2 Corinthians 13:14, NIV). The more we know Him, the more we know the Father and the Son. And the Holy Spirit never exalts Himself but always glorifies and magnifies the Lord Jesus. The Lord Jesus said of the Holy Spirit: *"He will glorify Me, for*

He will take of what is Mine and declare it to you" (John 16:14, NKJV). The Holy Spirit does not seek His own glory, nor does He want to draw attention to Himself, but to Jesus.

I like what R. A. Torrey said: "If the Holy Spirit is thought of as an impersonal influence or power, as so many do, then we rob Him of the worship that is His due, of the love that is His due, and of the faith and confidence and surrender and obedience that are His due."[1] This same Holy Spirit longs to reveal Jesus to you and empower you to love Him with all your heart, soul, and strength. But for that to happen, you must welcome Him into your life.

There is no greater way to express our love to the Lord than to surrender to His Holy Spirit every day. In fact, it is absolutely essential if you are to know the Person of the Holy Spirit intimately and experience His work profoundly. But surrender is only possible through prayer and brokenness before the Lord.

People often ask me, "Can anyone experience the Holy Spirit in such a deep way? Can anyone see the Holy Spirit do miraculous things?" The answer is absolutely yes! There is no special gift involved, only brokenness and surrender. So the question is not, do I have the gift? The question is, can I surrender all to Him?

Here is how the process begins. As you get to know the Lord, He begins to manifest Himself and His love for you. And a fellowship begins that grows and intensifies until you get to the place where you will say, "Lord Jesus, I give You my life, my mind, my heart, my dreams, my emotions, my thoughts; I give them all to You. I surrender spirit, soul, and body. Do with me as You will."

And as you surrender to Him, it is then that the Holy

Spirit begins to teach you, not just about yourself, but about all that the Father has for you. It is then that He imparts to you His strength and His living faith. For as Isaiah declared, *"In quietness and in confidence shall be your strength"* (Isaiah 30:15).

Everything about the Word of God now becomes stronger, and everything about prayer now becomes richer. A passage of Scripture you have read many times becomes more powerful than ever because of the presence of the Holy Spirit. And a peace and tranquility will come into your life, and for the first time you will understand what the Lord Jesus meant when He said, *"My peace I give unto you"* (John 14:27). All that becomes yours because of the Holy Spirit.

The Holy Spirit is a Gentleman. He will not intrude into our lives or force His presence upon us. But He will stay ever so close to those who desire His company. We need to welcome the Holy Spirit into every area of our daily lives by allowing Him to do His work in us and through us—at home, on the job, in school, at church, wherever we are. His wonderful presence should grace our prayer closets, our Bible studies, our worship, and our relationships with other people.

He longs to become your closest Companion and Helper. But it is up to you to extend the invitation. You must welcome His presence in your life.

A Deeper Walk

You cannot appreciate a person's work until you understand who they are. The same is true of the Holy Spirit. The better you understand who He is as a Person, the more you will be able to understand, experience, and carry out His great

4

work. My prayer for you as you read this book is for you to understand the Holy Spirit more deeply through a study of His nature, His names, and His work. I also pray that you will learn how to move into a deeper relationship as He anoints your life more and more to accomplish the will of God, the Father.

The Word of God in John 16:7 declares, *"But I tell you the truth: It is for your good that I am going away. Unless I go away, the Counselor will not come to you; but if I go, I will send him to you"* (NIV). Imagine that! You have been given a Counselor.

R. A. Torrey said, "I take this as one of the most precious · promises in the Word of God: that another Person just as divine as Jesus . . . is by my side always."[2]

Join me now as we discover how to experience a deeper relationship with the blessed Holy Spirit. You can have an intimate relationship with Him starting today.

PART I

The
PERSON
of the
HOLY
SPIRIT

CHAPTER ONE

𝒜 DEEPER DIMENSION

Traveling around the world, I'm convinced that the church has never experienced such hunger for a deeper move of God than what we are seeing today. I have been ministering for over three decades, and I have never seen such a desire on the part of so many believers for the presence of the precious Holy Spirit.

According to everything I have read in the Word of God, hunger is the greatest sign of spirituality, and Jesus promised us that if we are hungry, He will fill us. In fact, Master Jesus said: *"Blessed are they which do hunger and thirst after righteousness: for they shall be filled"* (Matthew 5:6). Not only did He call those who are hungry "blessed," but He promised to fill them and use them.

I believe with all my heart that hunger for the presence of God is what brings revival and change, not only for each of us individually, but collectively for the church of Jesus Christ. It's the answer for the world, for until people know how much we care, they don't care how much we know. Caring begins with a life dedicated to service—to God and to others. The deeper the desire for service, the greater impact believers will see.

In fact, I heard a story once of a woman who came to a pastor and asked, "I really want to know God, and I want to

9

be used by Him. Will you please tell me what consecration to Christ and service for Him means?" The pastor reached over to a nearby shelf for a blank piece of paper. Holding it up for her to see, he said, "It is to sign your name at the bottom of this blank sheet, and throughout your life to let God fill in the page as He wants."

How many of us are willing to do that? I believe that sort of deeper dimension of service can only happen when we are hungering and thirsting after God.

Spiritual Hunger

Many years ago I heard that the day you quit being hungry is the day you begin to die. This is true even in the physical realm. So as long as we are hungry, we are alive. Hunger is a sign of life. There are three things we need to consider about spiritual hunger:

10

- **Only God can birth true hunger in the spirit.** It cannot be manufactured by the flesh.
- **Hunger drives believers to deeper dimensions of service to God and others.** It enables us to come into a stronger relationship with Him, and as we become closer to Him, we become more like Him.
- **Spiritual hunger creates great expectations.** It causes us to have a better understanding and vision for what God is doing all around us.

This is happening today, perhaps more so than at any time in the past. I see the Lord is giving His children a deeper hunger than at any time in my life. He is doing a mighty work among those who are seeking to be used by Him.

Why?

He is doing this to bring forth a new manifestation of the Holy Spirit and to touch more people than ever with His salvation and miracle-working power. God has called us to be part of this Great Commission.

Getting Started

God declared, *"Call to Me, and I will answer you, and show you great and mighty things, which you do not know"* (Jeremiah 33:3, NKJV). In that powerful verse God promised three results to a man or woman who seeks more of God:

- **Revelation** (*"I will answer you."*)
- **Vision** (*"I will . . . show you."*)
- **Knowledge** (*". . . great and mighty things, which you do not know."*)

How would your life change if you had a greater revelation of God's purpose in your life?

How would your heart be transformed if you possessed more of His vision for reaching the world with the Gospel?

Can you imagine how effective you could be in doing God's will if you were filled with more and more of His knowledge?

It is possible for you to go deeper with the Holy Spirit. In fact, look at that passage in Jeremiah 33 again, and you will see that revelation, vision, and knowledge (verse 3) are just the beginning. Continuing, the Lord also offers these promises to believers who seek His face:

- I will bring health (verse 6).
- I will cure them (verse 6).
- I will reveal peace and truth (verse 6).
- I will pardon all their iniquities (verse 8).

- I will give goodness and prosperity (verse 9).
- I will bring righteousness (verse 16).

Obviously, there is much more to the Christian life than many of us have experienced. None of us have to stay that way. We are called to go deeper with Him. Much deeper!

Deeper Dimensions

What the Lord has prepared for those who love Him is beyond human comprehension. It cannot be seen with the eye or heard with the ear: *"But God hath revealed them unto us by his Spirit: for the Spirit searcheth all things, yea, the deep things of God"* (1 Corinthians 2:10). Seven deeper dimensions of the wonders of heaven can be yours through a closer, more powerful relationship with the Holy Spirit:

12

1. Desire

As a young Christian, I remember being active in a prayer group with a man who prayed the same prayer week after week, the same words, the same phrases. He was sincere, but after a few weeks I said to myself, here he goes again. I could almost recite his prayer for him! It was the same thing time after time.

Your first step in approaching God needs to be, "Lord, help my relationship with You, Your Son, and Your precious Holy Spirit to be fresh and alive, not merely a lot of rituals that I do out of a sense of responsibility." Suddenly, you move from the natural to the supernatural, and three things begin to happen inside:

- Your heart will be prepared by the Spirit.
- He will bring the Word to your remembrance.

- You'll begin to live and serve Him from your heart and spirit, not your mind.

In the land of Judah *"they had sworn with all their heart, and sought him with their whole desire; and he was found of them"* (2 Chronicles 15:15).

Spiritual hunger precedes personal revival. From our soul, we need to say as the psalmist, *"Lord, all my desire is before thee; and my groaning is not hid from thee"* (Psalm 38:9). Oh, what a transformation you'll experience when you begin to seek God's power in your life out of desire, not duty.

2. Diligence

We must grow in Christ through a greater desire, but we cannot totally forgive duty and diligence. They can go hand in hand.

Have you ever told the Lord, "Starting tomorrow, I'm going to get up one hour earlier every day so I can pray and read the Word." You may keep that vow for a day, a week, or even a month, but then what happens? Good intentions are somehow forgotten as you press the snooze button on your alarm and turn over and go back to sleep instead of getting up to spend time in God's presence.

There is only one way to enjoy a deeper dimension with the Holy Spirit: You must make spending time with Him a permanent part of your life. This includes reading the Word. It certainly means prayer. You can begin by making a commitment to God that allows no turning back. When the process begins you may have to tell yourself, "I'm going to make time for my Father whether I feel like it or not."

13

Then, as the days turn into months, you will discover that prayer, Bible study, service, and a deeper relationship with the Holy Spirit all become as natural and necessary as eating three "squares" a day. Without knowing when it happened, your diligence has transformed your time with the Holy Spirit into a positive habit, and that practice becomes a permanent part of your daily schedule.

Here is the Lord's message to you: *"I love them that love me; and those that seek me early [diligently], shall find me"* (Proverbs 8:17).

3. Truth

The person who talks with God only on Sunday doesn't understand what it means to have a deep, open, honest relationship with the Lord. It is through daily, constant communion that we move to a level of fellowship based on absolute truth and trust. The psalmist David asked:

> *Who shall ascend into the hill of the LORD? Or who shall stand in his holy place? He that hath clean hands, and a pure heart; who hath not lifted up his soul unto vanity, nor sworn deceitfully. He shall receive the blessing from the LORD, and righteousness from the God of his salvation.* (Psalm 24:3-5)

The searchlight of heaven sees through every pretense. Jesus declared: *"But the hour cometh, and now is, when the true worshippers shall worship the Father in spirit and in truth; for the Father seeketh such to worship him. God is Spirit: and they that worship him must worship him in spirit and in truth"* (John 4:23-24).

What happens to the person who attempts to fool God? The Lord says: *"I know thy works, that thou art neither cold nor*

hot: I would thou wert cold or hot. So then because thou art luke-warm, and neither cold nor hot, I will spue thee out of my mouth" (Revelation 3:15-16).

If you want to experience closeness to God and depth in your relationship with Him, you must allow honesty to rule your heart, for *"the LORD is nigh unto all that call upon him, to all that call upon him in truth"* (Psalm 145:18).

4. The Holy Spirit

Through a deeper walk with the Holy Spirit, you can experience a prayer language that allows you to speak directly to the Father. The apostle Paul wrote: *"For he that speaketh in an unknown tongue speaketh not unto men, but unto God: for no man understandeth him; howbeit, in the spirit he speaketh mysteries"* (1 Corinthians 14:2).

Paul cherished this private communication with the Father and said, *"I thank my God, I speak with tongues more than ye all"* (1 Corinthians 14:18). As you seek a deeper dimension with God, there are five reasons for praying in a heavenly language:

- **Praying in tongues builds you up.** *"He that speaketh in an unknown tongue edifieth himself"* (1 Corinthians 14:4). The Holy Spirit seeks to enlighten and instruct you in the deeper things of God.
- **Praying in tongues prepares you to prophesy**. Paul wrote, *"I would that ye all spake with tongues, but rather that ye prophesied"* (1 Corinthians 14:5). The word rather is translated "in order that." Tongues aid in proclaiming the Word and the prophecy.
- **Praying in tongues allows you to worship in a much deeper dimension.** Paul says, *"I will pray with the spirit,*

15

and I will pray with the understanding also: I will sing with the spirit, and I will sing with the understanding also" (1 Corinthians 14:15).

- **Praying in tongues brings rest when you are weary.** Isaiah wrote, *"For with stammering lips and another tongue will he speak to this people. To whom he said, 'This is the rest with wherewith ye may cause the weary to rest'"* (Isaiah 28:11-12).
- **Praying in tongues brings refreshing.** Isaiah, stating that God will use tongues to speak to His people, says, *"This is the refreshing"* (Isaiah 28:12).

5. Discipleship

I can trace my own deeper relationship with the Holy Spirit back to 1973, after attending a Kathryn Kuhlman meeting in Pittsburgh, Pennsylvania. It was the beginning of God's discipleship program for my life. Hour after hour, day after day, I prayed with my Bible open as the Spirit unveiled the truths of God's Word. The Holy Spirit promised to be my Counselor and Guide, and He has never, never disappointed me.

I discovered then that discipleship requires discipline in every area of your life. The Scripture shows us that after Pentecost those whom the Spirit had called continued *"daily with one accord in the temple"* (Acts 2:46). In another passage of Acts we read: *"Peter and John went up together into the temple at the hour of prayer, being the ninth hour"* (3:1).

Paul, who wrote a significant part of the New Testament, also understood discipleship and demonstrated what it meant to be a follower of Jesus. From experience and with authority he said, *"For this cause I bow my knees unto the Father of our Lord Jesus Christ"* (Ephesians 3:14). He prayed that we would know:

- **Strength:** *"That he would grant you, according to the riches of his glory, to be strengthened with might by his Spirit in the inner man"* (Ephesians 3:16).
- **Faith:** *"That Christ may dwell in your hearts by faith; that ye, being rooted and grounded in love"* (verse 17).
- **The fullness of God:** *"May be able to comprehend with all saints what is the breadth [width], and length, and depth, and height; and to know the love of Christ which passeth knowledge; that ye might be filled with all the fulness of God"* (verses 18-19).

It is through a deeper relationship with the Holy Spirit that we become the built-up, strong believers God wants us to be: *"But ye, beloved, building up yourselves on your most holy faith, praying in the Holy Ghost"* (Jude 20).

6. Freedom

In the city of Philippi, Paul and Silas were arrested for preaching the message of Christ. They were brought before the magistrates who *"rent [tore] off their clothes, and commanded to beat them. And when they had laid many stripes upon them, they cast them into prison"* (Acts 16:22-23). With chains tied to their feet *"at midnight Paul and Silas prayed, and sang praises unto God: and the prisoners heard them"* (16:25).

The Lord not only heard their prayer but moved heaven and earth on their behalf: *"And suddenly there was a great earthquake, so that the foundations of the prison were shaken: and immediately all the doors were opened, and every one's bands were loosed"* (16:26).

The Old Testament documents the fact that when God's people did not spend time seeking God, they were often subjugated and taken away like prisoners. On their journey *"the Assyrian oppressed them without cause"* (Isaiah 52:4). God looked down and said, *"Now therefore, what have I here . . . that my people is taken away for nought? they that rule over them make them to howl"* (verse 5).

Granted, most people live today without physically being bound, but more and more are finding themselves enslaved by "things," cares, addictions, and routine.

Are you ready for freedom rather than bondage, for deliverance rather than slavery, for joy rather than tears? Move into a deeper relationship with the Holy Spirit: *"Now the Lord is that Spirit: and where the Spirit of the Lord is, there is liberty"* (2 Corinthians 3:17).

7. A Heavenly Reward

18

As we move into a deeper relationship with the Holy Spirit, you also learn to set your *"affection on things above"* (Colossians 3:2). Paul tells us: *"Fight the good fight of faith, lay hold on eternal life, whereunto thou art also called, and hast professed a good profession before many witnesses. . . . Laying up in store for themselves a good foundation against the time to come, that they may lay hold on eternal life"* (1 Timothy 6:12, 19).

What a great moment to be alive, to enter a deeper relationship with the Holy Spirit, to build a powerful foundation that leads to an eternity in heaven! The great prophecies of Scripture are rapidly being fulfilled, and Jesus is coming back soon: *"But the end of all things is at hand: be ye therefore be sober [serious] and watch unto prayer"* (I Peter 4:7). We must be diligent in everything we do for Him. Jesus declared, *"Watch ye therefore, and pray always, that ye may be accounted worthy"* (Luke 21:36).

Can you imagine how wonderful heaven will be? As you seek more and more of Him in your life today, you are getting ready to spend forever and ever with Him!

Catching Up

The Bible declares that the natural man does not understand the things of God's Spirit, *"For they are foolishness unto him: neither can he know them, because they are spiritually discerned"* (1 Corinthians 2:14). The believer, however, is given a heavenly perspective: *"While we look not at the things which are seen, but at the things which are not seen: for the things which are seen are temporal; but the things which are not seen are eternal"* (2 Corinthians 4:18).

Today, as you seek more of God, ask Him to give you a greater thirst and hunger for a deeper relationship with the Holy Spirit which

- transports you from the limited to the unlimited,
- raises you from the earthly to the heavenly,
- lifts you from the natural to the supernatural,
- transforms you from the carnal to the spiritual,
- elevates you from the depths of destruction to the gates of glory,
- adds power and impact as you seek to serve Him, and
- breathes the Holy Spirit into every area of your life.

Once when the stress of administering a large ministry seemed overwhelming and I was caught up in details, I fell asleep from sheer exhaustion and had a dream. I saw Jesus walking and a large crowd was following Him. Then I heard His voice calling to me. He said, "Benny, you have some catching up to do." I saw myself running, getting closer to Jesus.

When I woke up I thought, "Lord, what does that mean?"

God spoke to me and said, "Get back to your calling. Get back to prayer and seeking a deeper walk with Me."

That morning I reaffirmed my commitment to obey God's mandate on my life, to take the message of God's saving and healing power to the world. I promised the Lord that I wouldn't let the details of the ministry distract me and keep me from doing what He had called me to do—to grow closer and closer to Him. And I have been faithful to that commitment. He continues to be faithful by multiplying my work for Him.

As Paul the apostle said, we must be *"redeeming the time, because the days are evil"* (Ephesians 5:16). The Lord desires your fellowship as you seek to be with Him and as you serve Him. He said to the prophet Malachi, *"Return unto me, and I will return unto you, saith the LORD of hosts"* (Malachi 3:7). The Lord is saying these same words to you and me today.

Have you spent time with Jesus today, or is there a need for some "catching up"?

Don't allow one more day to speed by without committing your heart, your time, your energy, and your service to Him. Treasure every moment with Him. If you have not been in His presence lately, hear His voice saying, "Come back. Return to Me."

And after all is said and done, you will learn that the greatest blessing is not merely receiving from God. It is becoming the kind of person God can trust and use. As we seek and serve Him and move into a deeper relationship with Him, we can be part of reaching the world with the Gospel and preparing for His soon return.

He has no hands but our hands
    To do His work today;
He has no feet but our feet
    To lead people in His way;
He has no voice but our voice
    To tell ones how He died;
He has no help but our help
    To lead them to His side.[1]

CHAPTER TWO

The HOLY SPIRIT

s we read the Bible, we see many names that refer to God the Father, Jesus the Son, and the Holy Spirit. This variety of titles is not meant to cause confusion, but to accomplish just the opposite. They are intended to help us understand and experience the countless wonderful aspects of the triune God. They help reveal His character and His nature—as brilliant, as rich, and as multifaceted as a precious jewel.

God, the great *"I AM"* (Exodus 3:14), is referred to by many different names throughout the Bible, each with a specific meaning and application. For example, they range from *"the Almighty God"* (Genesis 17:1) to *"the most High"* (Psalm 91:9) to *"the LORD of hosts"* and *"the Holy One of Israel"* (Isaiah 54:5) to *"JAH"* (Psalm 68:4).

The name of the Lord *Jesus* is the Greek form of the Hebrew name Joshua, which means "Yahweh saves." And this is exactly what Yahweh, the Lord God, did for us through the shed blood of His Son, Jesus Christ. Throughout the pages of Scripture, we also see many other titles and names used for the Lord Jesus—from *"the Prince of Peace"* (Isaiah 9:6) the *"bread of life"* (John 6:48) to *"the light of the world"* (John 8:12) to *"the good shepherd"* (John 10:11).

Likewise, the Holy Spirit has a variety of names throughout Scripture. Rightly understood, these names help us know who He really is and what He can do in our lives. They provide tremendous insight into the will, ways, and work of the

Holy Spirit. I'd like to show you what these names mean to you and how you can experience the Holy Spirit more intimately as you come to understand Him through His names.

The Holy Spirit

Perhaps the most common name you will hear for the Holy Spirit is exactly that—the Holy Spirit. That is not only His predominant title but also a power-packed definition of who and what He is. He is Holy—not defiled or common, but possessing all the purity and holiness of God. He is also Spirit—not flesh, as humans are, nor having a physical body, but sharing the very invisible nature and essence of God.

Because of the incredible glory that envelopes me and floods my being when I am in the presence of the Holy Spirit, I find it difficult to put into words just how I feel when I am in His presence. Words seem inadequate and cheap when attempting to describe an experience of such incredible spiritual wealth. The dimension of His power and presence is beyond anything else I have ever experienced. The Holy Spirit can take an ordinary hotel room and transform it into a sacred cathedral by His very presence. He can take a massive arena or stadium designed for sporting events and transform it into the Holy of Holies—the place where God's presence resides and is manifested. And in the vast expanse of that arena, any individual who has been touched by the presence of the Holy Spirit can experience such dynamic fellowship and intimacy in that presence that all awareness of others fades in the light of His glory.

Indeed that is one of the functions of the Holy Spirit—to grace people and places with the glorious presence of God's holiness. And when that happens, time seems to stand still.

When the Holy Spirit descends during my private devo-

24

tional times or in my public ministry, I often think of Moses when he stood before the burning bush. He took off his shoes because God said, *"The place whereon thou standest is holy ground"* (Exodus 3:5). By the Holy Spirit, I am aware of the wonderful presence of God, right there in the room with me. The Holy Spirit is called Holy because He "is holy in Himself, quite apart from all evil."[1] He brings a sense of reverence and glory into the very atmosphere where He is.

Let's look at some of the specific places throughout Scripture where the third Person of the Trinity is referred to as the Holy Spirit or the Holy Ghost.

- The psalmist prayed, *"Take not thy holy spirit from me"* (Psalm 51:11).
- Mary became pregnant *"with child of the Holy Ghost"* (Matthew 1:18).
- Matthew said, *"He shall baptize you with the Holy Ghost, and with fire"* (Matthew 3:11).
- The Lord Jesus declared, *"If ye then, being evil, know how to give good gifts unto your children: how much more shall your heavenly Father give the Holy Spirit to them that ask him?"* (Luke 11:13).
- The apostles wrote, *"It seemed good to the Holy Ghost, and to us"* (Acts 15:28).
- Romans 1:4 also declares Him to be *"the spirit of holiness"* in a passage referring to the Holy Spirit's role in the resurrection of the Savior.

So we see that the Holy Spirit's name carries a wealth of meaning and importance for every believer. I encourage you to get to know Him as each of these names reveals Him. Pray for a deeper understanding of His holiness and of His spiritual nature, which enables Him to be with you wherever you are, whenever you need Him.

CHAPTER THREE

The FATHER
and the
HOLY SPIRIT

In the Bible, we see at least sixteen names for the Holy Spirit that help define His relationship with the other Persons of the Trinity—the Father and the Son. Eleven of those sixteen relate specifically to the Father. Writes John Walvoord, "While there is some distinction in meaning in the various titles, the chief significance is to bring out the relationship of the Holy Spirit as the third person of the Trinity, all affirming His deity and procession."[1] Let's get to know Him better by looking carefully at each of these names.

The Spirit of God

The Spirit of God is the name of the Holy Spirit associated with power, prophecy, and guidance.

We first encounter the Spirit of God by this name in Genesis 1—the very first chapter of the Bible. At Creation, it was the Spirit of God who hovered over the face of the waters (see Genesis 1:2). Can you imagine the awesome power that was present when the universe was created? This mighty Spirit of God created all things from absolutely nothing!

Later, the New Testament tells a most remarkable story about what happened when the Lord Jesus healed a demon-possessed man who was also blind and deaf. The Pharisees accused Him of using satan's power to perform such a miracle. The Lord Jesus, who knew their thoughts, declared that He *"cast out devils by the Spirit of God"* (Matthew 12:28).

- Later, the same Spirit of God came upon Saul and caused him to prophesy (see 1 Samuel 10:10).
- He came upon Zechariah and enabled him to proclaim the Word of the Lord (see 2 Chronicles 24:20).
- Ezekiel's vision of the restoration of Israel was given *"by the Spirit of God"* (Ezekiel 11:24).

The Spirit of God is the Spirit of prophecy. He's the Spirit of power. And He is the Spirit of guidance. We see this as the Scripture declares in Romans 8:14: *"For as many as are led by the Spirit of God, they are the sons of God."*

Just think what it means to know that the Holy Spirit is dwelling within you—the same Holy Spirit who created the universe, the Holy Spirit who inspired prophecy, the Holy Spirit who cast out demons, and the same Spirit who raised Jesus Christ from the dead. He is living in your heart and making resurrection power available moment by moment. Hallelujah for the Spirit of God! And hallelujah that *"the Spirit of God dwelleth in you"* (1 Corinthians 3:16).

The Spirit of the Lord

We need to recognize that the Holy Spirit is much more than a representative of God, the Supreme Being. He is the Spirit of the Yahweh we worship, the Spirit of the I AM, the Spirit of the Lord of heaven and earth. This title for the Holy Spirit, the Spirit of the Lord, is used repeatedly in both the Old and New Testaments.

I love the story of Gideon. After years of oppression by the Midianites, Gideon answered God's call on behalf of the Israelites. Scripture tells us that *"The Spirit of the L*ORD* came upon Gideon,"* and he called his armies together (Judges 6:34). Thirty-two thousand men came to fight. The Lord told Gideon that there were too many men in the army. He did not want Israel to be able to brag about winning the battle because of their large number. He wanted them to be convinced that He alone had made them triumph and given them the victory.

So He asked Gideon to reduce the army to 300 men whose only weapons were a lamp and a trumpet. When these soldiers surrounded the vast armies of Midian and blew their trumpets, the enemy fled. It was the Spirit of the Lord who led Gideon to such a glorious triumph.

- Isaiah said, *"When the enemy shall come in like a flood, the Spirit of the L*ORD* shall lift up a standard against him"* (Isaiah 59:19).
- When the Lord Jesus began His ministry, He stood in the synagogue and quoted Isaiah saying, *"The Spirit of the L*ORD* is upon me"* (Luke 4:18).
- Paul used the same title to explain the workings of the mighty, victorious Spirit of the Lord, who uses His power to free us: *"Now the Lord is that Spirit and where the Spirit of the Lord is, there is liberty"* (2 Corinthians 3:17).

My Spirit

When God speaks of the Holy Spirit, He does it in a very personal way. He refers to Him as "My Spirit," clearly demonstrating the mystery of the Trinity and affirming that the Holy Spirit is a vital part of the Godhead. The Father, the Son, and the Holy Spirit are one God, yet they are three distinct personalities.

- God declared through Joel that in the last days before Christ's return, *"I will pour out my spirit upon all flesh"* (Joel 2:28).
- He also warned people everywhere in Genesis 6:3 to heed the Holy Spirit, saying, *"My spirit shall not always strive with man."*
- Zechariah reminded us that it is not by might or power, but *"by my spirit, saith the LORD of hosts"* (Zechariah 4:6).

The Spirit of the Living God

I love the work of the Holy Spirit. He makes God's Word so real *to* us and *in* us. The Scriptures associate the name Spirit of the Living God with the work of the Holy Spirit in making His Word come alive and in making His children *"living epistles"* (see 2 Corinthians 3:2-3). When we become living epistles, we are like a letter written to tell everyone about the goodness of God.

Instead of concentrating their efforts on being "living epistles" and giving the glory to the Lord, it is unfortunately true that sometimes some ministers may try to establish their importance by talking about the number of people in their church, the square footage of their buildings, the size of their mailing list, the number and size of their crusades, how many potential viewers exist for their broadcasts, how large their budget is, etc. But for me there is only one test, and it's very simple: Are lives changed? And how are lives changed? By the Spirit of the Living God.

Ledger sheets and membership rolls may be necessary for administration, but they are not important from an eternal perspective. People are important. And all that matters is that people are set free and able to enjoy abundant life by the Spirit of the living God. A person who is miraculously transformed by the Spirit of the living God is a living epistle —a walking, breathing testimonial of the power of the living God in the world today. Dear saint of God, I pray that you will go deeper with the Holy Spirit and begin to enjoy the highest level of liberation and abundance possible by the Holy Spirit. If you are not, all you need to do is ask. He is also your Helper, and He will set you in places of freedom and plenty that you have only dreamed of before.

Paul was so clear on this when some of the people at the church of Corinth questioned his credentials. His reply was simple: all of the people in the church at Corinth were his credentials because of the Spirit of the living God. Read what he wrote:

> Do we begin again to commend ourselves? or need we, as some others, epistles of commendation to you, or letters of commendation from you? Ye are our epistle written in our hearts, known and read of all men: Forasmuch as ye are manifestly declared to be the epistle of Christ ministered by us, written not with ink, but with the Spirit of the living God; not in the tables of stone, but in fleshly tables of the heart. And such trust have we through Christ to God-ward: Not that we are sufficient of ourselves to think any thing as of ourselves; but our sufficiency is of God; Who also hath made us able ministers of the new testament; not of the letter, but of the spirit: for the letter killeth, but the spirit giveth life. (2 Corinthians 3:1-6)

31

I believe you are longing, as I am, for a fresh anointing of the Spirit that will change your life and impact others through your walk with the Lord. Let us pray that we will be consumed by our longing to be used of God and to know His presence in a greater dimension than ever before.

The Power of the Highest

When I get to heaven, there are many people and heroes of the faith whom I want to meet. Mary, the mother of Jesus, is one of those individuals. In all of history, she alone encountered "the power of the Highest" in a way that has never been experienced before or since.

I want to know what it was like to experience God's power in the way Mary did. Oh, how I wish even now to sit with the great prophets of the Old Testament and discover things I am so hungry for. How I wish I could sit with Peter and ask him about the experience he had when his very shadow healed the sick; or with Paul who, when God's presence descended so strongly upon him, he was caught up to the third heaven. But Mary's experience with the Holy Spirit stands out as one of the greatest in Scripture.

As you know, one of the great central teachings and prophecies of Scripture is that the Messiah would be born of a virgin: *"Therefore the Lord himself shall give you a sign; Behold, a virgin shall conceive, and bear a son, and shall call his name Immanuel"* (Isaiah 7:14).

When Mary learned from the angel Gabriel that she would bear the Messiah, she asked the natural question: *"How shall this be, seeing I know not a man?"* (Luke 1:34).

Scripture records Gabriel's powerful reply, *"The Holy Ghost shall come upon thee, and the power of the Highest shall overshadow thee: therefore also that holy thing which shall be born of thee shall be called the Son of God"* (Luke 1:35).

Of course, that's exactly what happened. The impossible becomes possible when the power of the Highest comes.

Have you heard the story about the little boy who was trying to move a huge rock? He pulled and pushed, straining with all his might against this great rock. He even tried to move it with leverage from a board, but the rock would not budge.

His dad asked him, "Son, have you used all your resources?"

The son answered, "Yes, Dad. I've tried everything and I can't make it move."

His father replied, "No, you haven't. You haven't asked me to help you yet."

I know that you are hungry to see God's power transform your life, your relationships, and your work. Surrender anew to the Holy Spirit and invite the full measure of the power of the Highest to be unleashed in your life!

33

CHAPTER FOUR

JESUS CHRIST
the SON *and the* HOLY SPIRIT

We know that Jesus Christ is the Son of God. We know that, together, the Father, the Son, and the Holy Spirit comprise the Godhead, or the Trinity. As I explained the names of the Holy Spirit, I want to help you understand this wonderful mystery of the triune God. Now that you have read about the Holy Spirit's relationship to God the Father, let's look at the way He relates to Jesus the Son.

35

The Spirit of Christ

I once took a ski trip to the breathtaking Rocky Mountains in Colorado. The best part of the whole experience was the lift ride to the top—the beautiful snow-covered slopes below looked so peaceful and inviting. They gave no indication of the misery in store for an inexperienced skier (like I was) who actually tried to ski down from the summit. As the lift carried us higher and higher, I realized that what looked like a single mountain was actually a series of peaks, separated by valleys. Looking at the mountains from the ground, I could not tell where one started and another ended. Only when I got closer to the peaks did this become clear.

Similarly, long before the Lord Jesus Christ came to live

on earth, the prophets foretold the majestic mountaintop experience of salvation He would bring. They saw the two great peaks of Bible prophecy. They believed Christ would come to earth as the suffering Messiah, and also as the conquering Messiah. Yet from their perspective, the foretold events regarding the coming Messiah appeared as one mountaintop to the prophets of old. Although they saw His two great missions—suffering for the sins of mankind and conquering this fallen world—I'm sure they did not always understand the full significance and meaning of the words they spoke and were unclear as to when these events would actually occur.

I think this is what Peter wrote about when he declared, *"Of which salvation the prophets have enquired and searched diligently, who prophesied of the grace that should come unto you: Searching what, or what manner of time the Spirit of Christ which was in them did signify, when it testified beforehand of the sufferings of Christ, and the glory that should follow"* (1 Peter 1:10-11). The title, the Spirit of Christ, is so interesting here in this prophetic passage because it is a reminder of several things. I want to emphasize two of them.

First, it reminds us that the Spirit of the Lord inspired the human authors of Scripture: *"For prophecy came not in old time by the will of man: but holy men of God spake as they were moved by the Holy Ghost"* (2 Peter 1:21). Related to this is the clear testimony of the Word that the work of the Holy Spirit is to lift up the Lord Jesus Christ. The Lord Jesus said, *"He shall testify of me"* (John 15:26).

Second, it reminds us that the Scriptures focus on Jesus Christ. *"The testimony of Jesus is the spirit of prophecy"* (Revelation 19:10). Prophecy is all about the Lord Jesus, so when the Spirit of the Lord is involved with prophecies and prophets, He is working to proclaim the message of the Lord Jesus.

The Spirit of Jesus Christ

Philippians is such a marvelous book! Written from a dark, damp Roman prison cell, Paul teaches us in this book how we can have joy in spite of the place we're in, the people we're with, or the person we are. That's pretty remarkable when you think about it. Just about every challenge we face comes from one of these areas. How could Paul be so confident of joyful living in the midst of challenging circumstances? After all, he was in prison, shackled to a Roman soldier twenty-four hours a day. And in the midst of this, his reputation was being attacked by fellow believers. He himself gives us the answer: *"For I know that this shall turn to my salvation through your prayer, and the supply of the Spirit of Jesus Christ"* (Philippians 1:19).

37

Part of the great comforting work of the Holy Spirit is to give us peace and even joy in situations like these. In the context of Paul's book about joy, it makes sense that he would identify the connecting link to joy as the Spirit of Jesus Christ. After all, the Lord Jesus wanted our joy to be full and complete (see John 16:24) and, just before He was crucified, He prayed for the Father to send *another* Helper to abide with us and make our joy complete. The Holy Spirit that Jesus prayed for is the One who truly does bring the joy that the Savior wanted each of us to have.

So you see, joy comes through the Spirit of Jesus Christ regardless of our circumstances. The joy that you want, the joy that you are so diligently searching for, the joy that your spirit is crying out for only truly comes from one Person: the Spirit of Jesus Christ.

The Spirit of His Son

"And because ye are sons, God hath sent forth the Spirit of his Son into your hearts, crying, Abba, Father. Wherefore thou art no more a servant, but a son; and if a son, then an heir of God through Christ" (Galatians 4:6-7).

If you've read any of my previous books or been present in any of my services, you've probably heard me talk about my earthly father. The best way I can describe the way our father ran our family is to ask you to remember the father in the movie *The Sound of Music*. Except for the location and the singing, our house functioned much like the Von Trapp household did—strict discipline, well-understood instructions, comprehensive rules, everything neat and tidy, and plenty of work to do. When we failed to live up to the standards set for us, swift punishment was sure. Our home was run with military-like discipline. My brothers and sisters and I were even dressed in matching uniforms.

A former boxer, my father was a 6'2", 260-pound powerhouse. But even that doesn't begin to describe him. By virtue of his commanding personality, he really was larger than life. And there was never any doubt that he was in charge.

In his own way, he loved us. And I never doubted his love for any of us, even though I don't remember hearing him express it audibly very often until the very end of his life. For nearly the first thirty years of my life, my father's stern ways, combined with his type of personality, presented him as detached, distant, and somewhat cold emotionally. I don't think he was intentionally that way, but by his very makeup he was undemonstrative. And my speech impediment didn't make communicating with him any easier.

Although I was his firstborn son and I grew up under the same roof, ate bread from his table, and enjoyed the physical provision he made for our family, I never really knew what it was to have a close relationship with him until I was an adult. It wasn't until he was born again that I experienced the relationship that I had always longed for.

Knowing that, can you imagine the joy I experienced when I met the Lord and instantly felt a tremendous intimacy and affection with my heavenly Father? What took me thirty years to experience with my earthly father took me less than thirty seconds to experience with my heavenly Father.

I will never, ever lose my appreciation for the relationship the Holy Spirit gives me with the Father because of the sacrifice of the Lord Jesus. I'm no longer a slave to sin and alienated from the Father. I'm not in the Father's family as a stepchild—emotionally distant and never really accepted. I've been adopted as a full-fledged son and joint-heir, and so I can cry out, "Abba, Father!" (see Galatians 4:6). All of these benefits are yours, too, through the precious Holy Spirit.

I want you to understand that *abba* is an Aramaic term that small children would use in addressing their father, like "daddy" or "papa." The term is polite and intimate, even tender. And how can it be that we can have this kind of relationship with the Father? *"God hath sent forth the Spirit of his Son into [our] hearts, crying 'Abba, Father'"* (Galatians 4:6). Oh, my friend, come to know the Lord as your Abba today.

39

CHAPTER FIVE

The HOLY SPIRIT and YOU

You have seen how the Holy Spirit works in relation to the Father and to the Son. Now, I hope you have a better understanding of the way the Trinity functions. But there is one more important relationship that the Holy Spirit enjoys—His relationship with you!

The Spirit of Adoption

Something wonderful happens the moment we believe on Jesus Christ as our Savior. We are adopted into God's family. Instantly, we are given power to become children of God (see John 1:12). It is a fulfillment of the Father's great plan. He called us to *"adoption of children by Jesus Christ to himself, according to the good pleasure of his will"* (Ephesians 1:5).

Who arranges for our adoption? The Holy Spirit. Paul writes, *"For as many as are led by the Spirit of God, they are the sons of God. For ye have not received the spirit of bondage again to fear; but ye have received the Spirit of adoption"* (Romans 8:14-15).

The concept of adoption points to two great truths, both conveyed by the Holy Spirit. The first one is mentioned above. It is the great fact of our adoption into God's family with all the rights, privileges, and responsibilities that are a part of being a member of the family.

The second one is the great fulfillment of adoption—the transformation of our bodies at the Rapture when we receive the promised inheritance: *"And not only they, but ourselves also, which have the firstfruits of the Spirit, even we ourselves groan within ourselves, waiting for the adoption, to wit, the redemption of our body"* (Romans 8:23).

The most wonderful miracle we have ever seen won't compare to that great miracle of the Rapture when we'll exchange our mortal bodies for immortal bodies—bodies that will never be subject to sickness, disease, or death. Don't get me wrong, until that day everyone should absolutely seek their miracle from the Lord. You may be wondering, what is the foretaste or firstfruits of this great miracle to come? The Spirit of adoption! When will our adoption be culminated? When our bodies are redeemed at the Rapture. What a glorious day! Come quickly, Lord Jesus!

The Spirit of Glory

42

It seems more and more evident to me that Christians are coming under attack—especially in North America. I also see these attacks increasing in intensity. That's why I believe in what I call "violent faith"—faith that isn't passive, that doesn't tiptoe around, that isn't afraid of what people think, or that does not fear the consequences of being aggressive.

Peter wrote his first epistle to believers in Asia Minor who were experiencing the sting of persecution. He strongly and boldly declared, *"If ye be reproached for the name of Christ, happy are ye; for the spirit of glory and of God resteth upon you"* (1 Peter 4:14).

The Holy Spirit, speaking through Peter, gave these courageous believers two great assurances as they endured persecution. First, He assured them that they hadn't done anything wrong or believed anything wrong. Instead, their persecution showed that the very Spirit of the Lord rested upon them.

Second, He promised these brave believers that His glory would rest on them. He was talking about the magnificent glory of God—the same glory that the nation of Israel experienced in the wilderness and appeared as a cloud by day and the pillar of fire by night; the same glory that the high priest experienced in the Holy of Holies; the same glory that appeared to the shepherds keeping watch the night the Lord Jesus was born; the same glory that came upon the apostles in the Upper Room. This is the same glory that will be ours forever when we allow that glory to strengthen us.

Now believe me, I'm no stranger to persecution. When I trusted Christ, my whole family turned against me and ostracized me. But as I held firm, the Holy Spirit came upon me with His glory, energizing my spirit and giving me the strength to go on. Soon my entire family came to know Christ as Savior. For each of you who feels he is standing alone in the midst of opposition, take heart—the Holy Spirit of glory has promised to rest on *you* and He *will* keep His promise!

The Spirit of Grace

Have you taken time lately to reflect on the wonder of salvation? Without salvation, we would still be *"without Christ, being aliens from the commonwealth of Israel, and strangers from the covenants of promise, having no hope, and without God in the world"* (Ephesians 2:12). It is God's grace, His kindness, and undeserved favor that reached out to us. Even when we were His enemies He saved us. His amazing grace covered our guilt with His righteousness. His grace keeps us, for we were saved by grace through faith and kept by grace through faith. His grace brings us to the foot of the cross, unable to brag, able simply to say that our best was as filthy rags in His sight. His grace not only covers our failures—it transforms them into distinctive points of power and ministry[1]

Because of His grace, He gifts us and enables us to experience the joy of service and the delight of laboring with the Savior as He builds His church. Because of His grace, He puts resurrection power at our disposal, allowing us to persevere and prevail. Because of His grace, He rewards us, even in our unworthiness. Because of His grace, He indwells us, allowing us to experience the richness of moment-by-moment fellowship with the Spirit of the Lord. Because of His grace, He is returning for us, to transform us and allow us to experience the wonder of all He has prepared for us.

As Paul reflected on God's grace in salvation, he couldn't help but break out in a hymn of praise for God's grace in executing His plan of redemption:

> *O the depth of the riches both of the wisdom and knowledge of God! how unsearchable are his judgments, and his ways past finding out! For who hath known the mind of the Lord? or who has been his counselor? Or who hath first given to him, and it shall be recompensed unto him again? For of him, and through him, and to him, are all things: to whom be glory for ever. Amen.*
> (Romans 11:33-36)

How marvelous is the grace of God! And who do you suppose conveys this grace to us? The Holy Spirit. He is the very Spirit of grace and He ministers the Lord's grace to us moment by moment.

Yet, incredibly, some people feel the temptation to abandon the cause of Christ, to forsake the streams of living water for dry, empty creekbeds. The book of Hebrews was written, in part, to convince these people not to forsake the Lord. The Scripture declares:

He that despised Moses' law died without mercy under two or three witnesses: Of how much sorer punishment, suppose ye, shall he be thought worthy, who hath trodden under foot the Son of God, and hath counted the blood of the covenant, wherewith he was sanctified, an unholy thing, and hath done despite unto the Spirit of grace? (Hebrews 10:28-29)

Rejecting God's law brought swift and thorough judgment in Old Testament days. How much more, then, should we fear the consequences of holding in contempt the Son of God, His sacrifice, the Spirit of God, and His grace? The Father will not take lightly the despising of the Son and the Spirit. He warns us plainly in His Word: "It is *a fearful thing to fall into the hands of the living God*" (Hebrews 10:31).

The Spirit of Grace and of Supplication

45

There are some people who minimize the importance of Bible prophecy, and even some who make fun of it. Mark Twain said, "If the world comes to an end, I want to be in Cincinnati—things always come twenty years later in Cincinnati." But it's important to realize that 25 percent of the Bible is prophetic in nature—an amount equal in size to the entire New Testament. Do you think God would devote 25 percent of His Word to an unimportant subject? I certainly do not.

I am waiting and watching for the Rapture, the inauguration of so many of the great prophetic events of Scripture. Martin Luther, the father of the Protestant Reformation, said he only had two days on his calendar—today and "that day!"[2] That's the way I want to be, too! I want to live today for "that day!"

One of the great prophetic passages of Scripture is Zechariah 12. It describes the reconciliation of the Jewish people with the Savior they rejected. This great event occurs at the second coming of Christ. Try to imagine the profound emotion of this moment.

On the one hand is the Lord Jesus, the rejected King, now returned as Conqueror. The One who said with such emotion, *"O Jerusalem, Jerusalem, thou that killest the prophets, and stonest them which are sent unto thee, how often would I have gathered thy children together, even as a hen gathereth her chickens under her wings, and ye would not!"* (Matthew 23:37).

On the other hand is the Jewish nation. They have lived through the horrors of the Tribulation. They have seen the awesome power of the glorified Savior returning to earth with His armies to destroy His enemies. And now in a moment of time they realize that the One they had so steadfastly rejected is the precious Son of God and they turn to Him in faith. Who prepared the way for this reconciliation? The Holy Spirit!

More than five hundred years before Christ, the Lord described this scene to the prophet Zechariah: *"And I will pour upon the house of David, and on the inhabitants of Jerusalem, the spirit of grace and of supplications: and [or "so that" in the NASB] they shall look upon me whom they have pierced, and they shall mourn for him, as one mourneth for his only son, and it shall be in bitterness for him, as one that is in bitterness for his firstborn"* (Zechariah 12:10).

When the Lord poured out His Spirit upon His battered and bedraggled people, He broke through their resistance so they could experience God's favor (grace), and that freed their hearts to call out to Him in repentance.

Supplication, as it is used here to describe the Holy Spirit refers "less [to a] formal entreaty . . . than the outpourings of a troubled soul."[3] That's what the Holy Spirit does. No matter what we've done or how we have failed, He helps us come to the Father in freedom and find the forgiveness and mercy so abundantly available to all.

The Spirit of Wisdom and Understanding

Isaiah 11 is one of those mountaintop passages of Scripture— so powerful and moving. As Isaiah describes the coming of the Messiah in verse 2 of this great chapter, he uses a series of three couplets to describe the work of the Holy Spirit in the life and ministry of Christ Jesus:

> *The spirit of wisdom and understanding*
>
> *The spirit of counsel and might*
>
> *The spirit of knowledge and of the fear of the* LORD

As part of the Godhead, one of the attributes of the Holy Spirit is that He is unchanging. You can always, always count on Him because He stays the same. Because of His constancy, we can expect that the Holy Spirit will make manifest these same qualities in us as we allow Him to work.

"*The spirit of wisdom and understanding*" (Isaiah 11:2). Wisdom is nothing more than living with skill. It goes beyond intellectual knowledge to include the ability to apply the knowledge of God's Word in our daily life—and nothing less. It involves using knowledge in the right way to select the right ends. Then wisdom directs us to achieve those ends in a proper fashion. It involves applying God's truth to human experience. Properly mastered, it can lead to a happy and successful life.

This skillful living manifested itself in the life of the Lord Jesus even from His childhood. As a child, Jesus was "*filled with wisdom*" and "*increased in wisdom*" (Luke 2:40, 52).

Wisdom was also evident in His preaching: "*And when the sabbath day was come, he began to teach in the synagogue:*

and many hearing him were astonished, saying, From whence hath this man these things? and what wisdom is this which is given unto him, that such mighty works are wrought by his hands?" (Mark 6:2). They marveled at the wisdom of His words, and at the practical skill His words imparted. And did you notice the connection they made between the wisdom of His teaching and His mighty works: *"wisdom . . . that such mighty works are wrought by his hands!"* Wisdom is about actions as well as words.

And because godly wisdom is so rare, the wisdom of Jesus's actions routinely baffled and angered those without this wisdom. The Lord Jesus recounted the words of His critics: *"The Son of man came eating and drinking, and they say, Behold a man gluttonous, and a winebibber, a friend of publicans and sinners. But wisdom is justified of her children"* (Matthew 11:19). And the mighty, Spirit-led growth of the church, growing in every continent and country, every village and community and country bears ample testimony to the wisdom of the Master's strategy. *"But wisdom is justified of all her children"* (Luke 7:35). In other words, wisdom is proven by the right actions of those who practice it.

Understanding is the same as having discernment in wisdom. It is not about the accumulation of facts. The idea here is that a person with understanding has the insight to choose with skill between the options that come his way. "*Bin* [the Hebrew word for "understanding" in Isaiah 11] is the power of judgment and perspective insight and is demonstrated in the use of knowledge."[4]

This kind of perception comes from the Holy Spirit, but not automatically. We must diligently seek it. Proverbs, known as the "book of wisdom," puts it this way:

My son, if thou wilt receive my words, and hide my commandments with thee; So that thou incline thine ear unto wisdom, and apply thine heart to understanding; Yea, if thou criest after knowledge, and liftest up thy voice for understanding; If thou seekest her as silver, and searchest for her as for hid treasures; Then shalt thou understand the fear of the LORD, and find the knowledge of God. For the LORD giveth wisdom: out of his mouth cometh knowledge and understanding. (Proverbs 2:1-6)

Since this understanding comes from God alone, the wicked are infamous for their lack of ability to perceive the wisdom of the Lord: *"The righteous considereth the cause of the poor: but the wicked regardeth not to know it "* (Proverbs 29:7).

What an incredible comfort these words are for the righteous! There are many choices, alternatives, and options in the world. Sometimes it seems impossible to choose between them. Thanks be to God that, through the Holy Spirit, we can have *wisdom* (skill in living life), and *understanding* (discernment to choose between the alternatives we face).

With the counsel and might of the Holy Spirit in our hearts and minds, our perspective is fresh and full of insight, and our outlook is optimistic. But without it, this present existence is at best dark, dreary, and depressing. Bertrand Russell, one of the foremost atheists of our time, described his perspective on life this way:

49

The life of man is a long march through night surrounded by invisible foes, tortured by weariness and pain, toward a goal that few can hope to reach and where none can tarry long. One by one as they march, our comrades vanish from our sight, seized by the silent orders of omnipotent death. Brief and powerless is man's life. On him and all his race the slow sure doom falls, pitiless and dark. Blind to good and evil, reckless of destruction, omnipotent matter rolls on its relentless way. For man, condemned today to lose his dearest, tomorrow himself to pass through the gates of darkness, it remains only to cherish, ere the blow falls, the lofty thoughts that ennoble his little day.[5]

The Spirit of Counsel and Might

In the second of the three couplets, Isaiah describes the Holy Spirit as *"the spirit of counsel and might"* (Isaiah 11:2).

I'm so glad the Holy Spirit as our Counselor gives us the meaning and fulfillment in life which Bertrand Russell so desperately needed. There is no doubt that his is the way the ungodly view life. It is bankrupt and utterly meaningless for them.

50

As the prophet Isaiah emphasized, the Holy Spirit was *"the spirit of counsel and might."* In Isaiah 11:2, he is prophesying again about the coming of the Lord Jesus. It is the counsel and might of the Holy Spirit in the mystery of the Trinity that allow the Lord Jesus to be called *"Wonderful, Counsellor"* and *"The mighty God"* (Isaiah 9:6). "The attributes of the Holy Spirit would characterize the Messiah. Because of His wisdom, understanding, counsel, and knowledge He is the Wonderful Counsellor" (see Isaiah 9:6).[6]

The Holy Spirit also delights to counsel us. He is not only able, but He really wants to help you. Quit trying to figure it out all by yourself and let the Holy Spirit counsel you! Stop trying to muster the power to push your way through things. With the Holy Spirit, your motto can be, "Not somehow, but triumphantly!"

We have the great resources of the Holy Spirit at our disposal, and yet some of us live our lives in spiritual poverty and frustration, not using the riches that are at our immediate beck and call. We simply need to go deeper. Not only does He give us guidance, but He imparts the strength and energy to carry out His plans. Remember, the Lord Jesus said, *"But ye shall receive power, after that the Holy Ghost is come upon you"* (Acts 1:8).

The Spirit of Knowledge and of the Fear of the Lord

The third couplet in Isaiah 11:2 describes the Holy Spirit as *"the spirit of knowledge and of the fear of the LORD."* He not only is that Spirit, He imparts *"knowledge and the fear of the Lord"* to us.

The word *knowledge* here refers to the knowledge we gain through our senses, both about how the world works and about God's moral law. Thus, the Holy Spirit gives us the ability to look at the world and perceive His handiwork and purposes in it. The Bible declares that *"the invisible things of him from the creation of the world are clearly seen, being understood by the things that are made, even his eternal power and Godhead"* (Romans 1:20). When we are in tune with the leading of the Holy Spirit, we gain a fuller understanding of the world around us, and every day can be packed with awe and wonder.

But not only does He bring knowledge, the Holy Spirit also brings *"the fear of the Lord."* This is so important to understand. Solomon, under the inspiration of the Holy Spirit, said, *"The fear of the LORD is the beginning of knowledge: but fools despise wisdom and instruction"* (Proverbs 1:7).

I don't want you to misunderstand my next thoughts. I'm

51

grateful for all the emphasis these days on spiritual warfare. I believe it has made us more sensitive to the spiritual struggles going on around us. But I fear that an unintended result of all this teaching is that men and women now fear the devil more than they fear God. I tell you, Fear God, and you will not need to fear the devil. You'll be aware of his power and act accordingly as the archangel Michael did (see Jude 8-9), but you will not fear the devil for *"greater is he that is in you, than he that is in the world"* (1 John 4:4).

By the way, there is a difference between fearing the Lord and being afraid. Exodus 19 and 20 show this so beautifully. The nation of Israel is gathered at Mount Sinai to enter into a covenant relationship with Yahweh and receive the Ten Commandments from Him. Mount Sinai was ablaze with *"thunders and lightnings, and a thick cloud [was] upon the mount, and the voice of the trumpet exceeding loud; so that all the people that was in the camp trembled"* (Exodus 19:16).

In fact, the nation of Israel said to Moses, *"Speak thou with us, and we will hear: but let not God speak with us, lest we die"* (Exodus 20:19).

Then Moses utters these remarkable words: *"Fear not: for God is come to prove you, and that his fear may be before your faces, that ye sin not"* (Exodus 20:20). He was saying, "Don't be afraid, but fear!" See the difference? The people were trembling at God's power. But what the Father wanted was for them to have a healthy respect of His power that would lead to a sense of awe which would then keep them from sinning. The *"fear of the Lord"* doesn't mean being afraid, it means understanding Him and respecting Him such that we live a life of loving obedience.

And who brings this ability to fear the Lord? The Holy Spirit!

The Spirit of Life

I love the words of the Lord Jesus, *"I have come that they might have life, and that they might have* it *more abundantly"* (John 10:10). Abundant life—there is something so compelling about that, something that says within us, "Yes, I must have this." And who ministers this abundant life to us? The Holy Spirit. The Lord Jesus said, *"It is the spirit that quickeneth; the flesh profiteth nothing: the words that I speak unto you, they are spirit, and they are life"* (John 6:63). Now the life He's talking about is salvation, but it is also true that "what God promises for eternity, he begins to do in this lifetime."[7]

Oh my dear friend, when the Spirit of the Lord comes, He brings *life*—breaking the power of canceled sin and death. Whatever has died in you can live again just by His touch! And He brings not just endless life, but better life right now. Paul says, *"The law of the Spirit of life in Christ Jesus hath made me free from the law of sin and death"* (Romans 8:2).

Are you experiencing all the life the Holy Spirit has for you? Someone gave me this quote, and I think it sums up the issue magnificently:

> I believe that only one person in a thousand knows the trick of really living in the present. Most of us spend fifty-eight minutes each hour either living in the past, regretting for lost joys, or feeling shame for things badly done (both utterly useless and weakening); or living the future which we either long for or dread. The only way to live is to accept each minute as an unrepeatable miracle, which is exactly what it is—a miracle that will not be repeated.[8]

The Spirit of the Lord is waiting just now to heal your past, guarantee your future, and liberate you to experience abundant life right now.

The Holy Spirit of Promise

Paul declared that those who trusted Christ as their Savior are *"sealed with the Holy Spirit of promise, which is the earnest of our inheritance"* (Ephesians 1:13-14). Please notice two things.

First, He is the *"Holy Spirit of promise."* That is, "the promised Spirit."[9] The Lord Jesus promised in the Upper Room Discourse that He would send the Holy Spirit, but the Lord Jesus made the promise in conjunction with the Father. He is called the Holy Spirit, the One, *"whom the Father will send in my name"* (John 14:26). He also said, *"I will send unto you from the Father, . . . which proceedeth from the Father"* (John 15:26). Thus the Holy Spirit was promised by the Father as well, and is termed in Acts 1:4 as *"the promise of the Father."* Because of their faith in the words of the Father and the Son, that early band in Jerusalem took God at His word and waited for the Holy Spirit. And God did not disappoint them.

54

Don't ever forget that *"God is not a man, that he should lie; neither the son of man, that he should repent: hath he said, and shall he not do* it? *or hath he spoken, and shall he not make it good?"* (Numbers 23:19). Some people would have you believe that God's Word, the Bible, isn't true, or isn't completely true. Regardless of how they articulate their words, what they're doing is calling each member of the Godhead a liar. It's an old saying but a true one: "God said it. I believe it. That settles it." And might I add, I'm going to live like it. Just like the expectant followers in the Upper Room, take Him at His word in *everything* He says.

Second, the indwelling of the Holy Spirit is a promise that one day we will receive all that has been promised and prepared for us: a new body, a new nature, and a new home. The Holy Spirit living within us is demonstrating, moment by moment, that God will one day present us with the full measure of our inheritance. That will be a wonderful day!

The Spirit of Truth

Another one of the great titles ascribed to the promise of the Father is the Spirit of truth. The Holy Spirit has a specific assignment from God to communicate and impart what is true and valid. The Lord Jesus described Him as *"the Spirit of truth; whom the world cannot receive, because it seeth him not, neither knoweth him: but ye know him; for he dwelleth with you, and shall be in you"* (John 14:17).

Not only does He teach truth, He *is* truth.

He will teach you the truth about Jesus (the direct meaning of John 14:17).[10]

He will teach you the truth about the *Bible*. The Lord Jesus declared, *"When he, the Spirit of truth, is come, he will guide you into all truth"* (John 16:13; see also 1 Corinthians 2:10-11).

He will teach you the truth about yourself. David was so refreshingly honest when he asked the Lord, *"Who can understand his errors? cleanse thou me from secret faults"* (Psalm 19:12). No one can fully discern his or her own errors, but as we listen to the voice of the Holy Spirit and follow His prompting, areas in our lives that are invisible to us will be refined and sublimated by the Holy Spirit. *"But we all, with open face beholding as in a glass the glory of the Lord, are changed into the same image from glory to glory, even as by the Spirit of the Lord"* (2 Corinthians 3:18).

The Comforter

If you have ever had to appear to defend yourself in court or before the government, you know what a harrowing experience it can be. Although our American justice system dictates that a person is innocent until proven guilty, that's rarely how an individual in that situation actually feels. What you feel is powerless, alone, and hurting. Oh, how you long for someone to help you bear the burden.

I have good news! In a spiritual sense, this is exactly what the Holy Spirit does. The Lord said, *"I will pray the Father, and he shall give you another Comforter, that he may abide with you for ever"* (John 14:16). Jesus, in this verse is promising another Comforter. The word *comforter* in the Greek language is *paraclete*—meaning, "one called alongside to help." In natural terms, a paraclete is like a defense attorney, an advocate, a helper who will fight your battles. In spiritual terms, the Holy Spirit does all this and more. He is a Helper who is so good at what He does that He calms your restless fears and stills your troubled heart.

Mere words are totally insufficient to express the depth of my love toward the Holy Spirit for the many ways and the many times He has helped me. He truly has been my constant Helper and Comforter. And when I stand before the people to preach the Gospel, He is there beside me, helping me. As Paul said, *"My speech and my preaching was not with enticing words of man's wisdom, but in demonstration of the Spirit and of power"* (1 Corinthians 2:4).

Praise God for our Comforter!

The Eternal Spirit

As a Person of the Godhead, the Holy Spirit was present before time, has been present in every moment in history, and will remain after, as the old hymn says, "time shall be no more."

The writer of the book of Hebrews recognized the Holy Spirit's eternal nature when he wrote that if the blood of bulls and goats was once used as a sacrifice, *"How much more shall the blood of Christ, who through the eternal Spirit offered himself without spot to God, purge your conscience from dead works to serve the living God?"* (Hebrews 9:14).

Just as the Melchizedekian priesthood of Christ is superior to the priesthood of the Old Testament, so the redemption effected through the eternal Spirit is superior to the temporary remedies of the law—remedies designed not so much to redeem man as to point out man's need for redemption through faith in Christ.

Saying that He is an "eternal" Spirit is the same as saying He is a "divine" Spirit. His existence is infinite. "The term *eternal*, which with all propriety can also be assigned to God the Father or God the Son, is here assigned to the Holy Spirit. Since to God alone this attribute may be predicated, the Spirit is understood as God."[11]

57

The Spirit

The Word of God gives many wonderful names to the Holy Spirit, but perhaps the most unadorned name is the most profound. He is often referred to in the Scriptures simply as "the Spirit."

That was the term John the Baptist used when he described what happened at the baptism of the Lord Jesus. He said, *"I saw the Spirit descending from heaven like a dove, and it abode upon him"* (John 1:32). You might even say, the Spirit, the unique Spirit, the one and only Spirit, for after all, in person, in work, and in our personal experience of His indwelling, there is none like Him.

The Lord Jesus also used the same words. He declared to Nicodemus, *"Except a man be born of water and of the Spirit, he cannot enter into the kingdom of God"* (John 3:5).

Again and again, we are encouraged to *"be filled with the Spirit"* (Ephesians 5:18; see Acts 9:17).

The names given to the Holy Spirit are significant and glorious. But they are not given simply that we may know *about* Him. They are names we can use every day to truly know Him and welcome Him into the very recesses of our lives.

Yes, He is the Spirit of the Father and the Son. But He is ready to be your Paraclete—your Counselor, your Helper, your Teacher, and your Guide. He is here to be the Spirit of glory and grace, the Spirit of wisdom and knowledge and might, the very Spirit of the living God and of Jesus Christ in your life today.

PART II

The
WORK
of the
HOLY
SPIRIT

CHAPTER SIX

ℐ*he* WORK
of the HOLY SPIRIT

N ow that you understand the Holy Spirit better because of His names, I want you to understand Him
better because of His work. One of the greatest
things the Holy Spirit does is to change people. He truly
does, my friend. He changes people from the inside out—
their lives, their circumstances, their perspectives. He will
change you, too.

You can find the work of the Holy Spirit in each of the
Bible's sixty-six books. The book of Acts is sometimes
called "The Acts of the Apostles." It is also referred to as
"The Acts of the Holy Spirit," and that's the way I like to
think of it. As you seek to go deeper in your walk with the
Spirit of God, I would like to take you through this wonderful book of Acts and show you, chapter by chapter,
exactly what He can do in your life as you grow in your
relationship with Him.

The book of Acts is a record of the dramatic changes
that happened in the lives of the apostles because of the fellowship of the Holy Spirit. When you welcome the Holy
Spirit into your life, the same things can happen to you. As
you read about the ways He can change you, pray to see
these promises become a reality for you.

Acts 1: He will change the way you hear.

Just before Jesus returned to heaven, He told His apostles not to leave Jerusalem, but to wait for *"the promise of the Father"* that He had spoken to them about (Acts 1:4). He said, *"For John truly baptized with water; but ye shall be baptized with the Holy Ghost not many days hence"* (Acts 1:5).

The Lord's instructions were somewhat difficult for the apostles to understand. They knew well the fellowship of Jesus and how to enjoy a relationship with Him, but they had no concept of what it meant to be baptized with the Spirit.

The Holy Spirit takes you beyond hearing with your ears and helps you listen with your heart. He gives you the understanding that comes from listening with your heart (spiritual hearing) in addition to the knowledge that comes from listening with your ears (physical hearing).

Acts 2: He will change the way you speak.

When the Holy Spirit came upon the apostles, He changed their speech as they *"began to speak with other tongues, as the Spirit gave them utterance"* (Acts 2:4).

With the power he received at Pentecost, Peter declared the message of Christ, and about three thousand people were added to the church in one day (see Acts 2:41).

Episcopalian Dennis Bennett, in his inspiring book *The Holy Spirit and You*, explains it well: "He overflowed from them out into the world around, inspiring them to praise and glorify God, not only in their own tongues, but in the new languages, and in so doing, tamed their tongues to His use, freed their spirits, renewed their minds, refreshed their bodies, and brought power to witness."[1]

Acts 3: He will change your appearance.

Here's what I notice about people with a strong anointing of the Holy Spirit on their lives. They look young, regardless of their age. Their eyes sparkle, and they have physical strength.

Years ago, I knew a minister whose countenance radiated with the presence of the Lord. I knew him for years, and he had a great anointing of the Spirit upon his life and ministry. During his ministry, however, a major problem surfaced in his life. Instead of dealing with it, he chose to ignore it, and the presence of God left him. I saw him only a few months later and was shocked! He didn't even look like himself. He appeared to be a haggard old man. His zeal for life had vanished. He had aged years in just a few months. And even more tragic than the physical changes in his appearance, the anointing of the Holy Spirit no longer rested upon him as it once had.

63

After Peter and John were filled with the Holy Spirit, they went to the temple gate and a beggar asked them for money. The first words they spoke to him were, *"Look on us"* (Acts 3:4). You see, they knew that a look of power and boldness had come upon them because of God's presence. They knew that the life of the Holy Spirit on the inside of them had changed the way they looked on the outside, and their whole countenance reflected an inner work of God's presence.

Instead of giving him money, Peter said, *"Silver and gold have I none; but such as I have give I thee: In the name of Jesus Christ of Nazareth rise up and walk"* (Acts 3:6).

The crippled beggar jumped to his feet and began running, leaping, and praising God. When the people saw what had occurred, *"they were filled with wonder and amazement at that which had happened unto him"* (Acts 3:10).

The presence of the Lord makes a difference in your life. The Holy Spirit even changes the way you look.

Acts 4: He will change your behavior.

I have great difficulty whenever I try to fully describe what I experience during a service when the anointing of the Holy Spirit comes upon me. I become bold against satan and all his forces. I become a different man—fearless and without apprehension. Everything changes in a moment's time, all because of the wonderful anointing of the Holy Spirit.

I know from personal experience that the Holy Spirit truly does change an individual's behavior as the anointing of the Holy Spirit anoints a man or woman of God for service. On many occasions I have watched a video from a miracle crusade service or a television broadcast from a similar event. Each time, I look on in total awe and wonder as I watch myself, the "Benny Hinn" on the television screen, as I minister with boldness and authority under the anointing of the Holy Spirit. I marvel at what I see myself do sometimes, for I know that it's the anointing of the Holy Spirit that makes the difference. It's an awesome experience, one that I treasure and thank the Lord for.

Because of the Holy Spirit, the behavior of Peter and John was drastically changed after the Day of Pentecost. Instead of fearing the Jews, they were proclaiming the message of the Gospel with confidence. *"Now when they saw the boldness of Peter and John, and perceived that they were unlearned and ignorant men, they marveled; and they took knowledge of them, that they had been with Jesus"* (Acts 4:13). Isn't that beautiful? Because of the change in these men, people realized *"that they had been with Jesus."*

A relationship with the Holy Spirit gives you, among

other gifts, three kinds of boldness: boldness to come before God, boldness with other people, and boldness against satan.

Who gave David the courage to do battle against Goliath? Who gave Paul the boldness to stand before King Agrippa and insist that Jesus is still alive? God's Holy Spirit.

He is still in the business of changing behavior.

Acts 5: He will change your experience.

Peter had a new friend who may have been invisible to others but was a reality to him. He told the Sanhedrin, the supreme Jewish court, *"We are his witnesses of these things; and so is also the Holy Ghost, whom God hath given to them that obey him"* (Acts 5:32).

The disciples did not say, "We are His witnesses" or, "So are the soldiers who were there." The Holy Spirit was real to them, and the evidence of His presence in their lives was there for all to see. *"God also bearing them witness, both with signs and wonders, and with divers miracles, and gifts of the Holy Ghost, according to his own will?"* (Hebrews 2:4). They were actually seeing part of the power that Jesus had promised to them before He ascended into heaven (see Acts 1:8).

Oh, how wonderful it is to have the Holy Spirit as your Friend and Companion and to experience His reality each and every moment. He will never, ever leave you!

Acts 6: He will change your position.

It is impossible to predict where your walk with the Holy Spirit will lead. The story of Stephen, as recorded in Acts, is a good example. He was not an apostle before becoming a deacon. Stephen was simply active in the church in Jerusalem, a man full of the Holy Spirit and of faith (see Acts 6:5).

65

It is apparent that the Holy Spirit was moving in a great and powerful way, touching not only the preachers but also the laymen, for the Bible says, *"Stephen, full of faith and power, did great wonders and miracles among the people"* (Acts 6:8).

How did he move from his position as a layman to a position in ministry as an usher or administrator, and then to an evangelist? He was moved because of his fellowship with the Holy Spirit. And because of this fellowship, the Holy Spirit gave him great authority and changed his position.

When members of the synagogue began to argue with Stephen, *"they were not able to resist the wisdom and the spirit by which he spake"* (Acts 6:10). He had a new position, and new authority in ministry. The beloved Holy Spirit can do the same for you.

Acts 7: He will change your vision.

A relationship with the Holy Spirit will change what you see and how you see. Instead of looking down, you'll start looking up—where the horizon is much brighter. You'll see things differently than you do now, and you'll understand things you never have before.

Stephen was about to be bound and carried through the streets of Jerusalem and stoned for his faith, but the Holy Spirit gave him a glorious vision. The Bible says that he, *"being full of the Holy Ghost, looked steadfastly into heaven, and saw the glory of God, and Jesus standing on the right hand of God"* (Acts 7:55).

To get a new perspective, follow the advice of Paul in Colossians 3:2: *"Set your affection on things above, not on things on the earth."* This is the kind of vision God desires for His people to have, and the Holy Spirit is able to impart it to you.

Acts 8: He will change your discernment.

Have you ever met a Christian who had no tact or wisdom when dealing with people who didn't know the Lord? I have, and I'll tell you, God is concerned with timing and with tact. He wants us to do things at the right time and in the right way.

When the perfect moment came to witness to an Ethiopian, *"The Spirit said unto Philip, Go near, and join thyself to this chariot. And Philip ran"* (Acts 8:29-30).

Philip knew the voice of God so well that when the Spirit said, "Now," Philip responded instantly and ran. He didn't want to miss the opportunity.

During Paul's journeys, he did not witness to people until they were ready for it. Once, when he was on a ship headed for Rome, a violent storm erupted. If he had witnessed to the unbelievers when there was no temptest in their life, they probably would have turned a deaf ear. Paul had the right words. But more than that, he was sensitive to discern the right time. He spoke of *"the angel of God, whose I am, and whom I serve, Saying, Fear not"* (Acts 27:23-24). He told them that God promised to protect all who sailed with him.

Don't trust your own judgment. Pray for the Holy Spirit to give you discernment; then follow His guidance. He will always lead you perfectly.

Acts 9: He will change your attitude.

Saul, who later was called Paul, is a prime example of the way the Holy Spirit can transform your walk. Can you imagine calling someone who is a blasphemer, a persecutor, and a murderer, "brother"?

To the natural ear, that sounds impossible. But that's what

the Holy Spirit can do. He makes the impossible possible. When God told Ananias to go and pray for Saul, he argued: *"Lord, I have heard by many of this man, how much evil he hath done to thy saints at Jerusalem"* (Acts 9:13).

Nevertheless, Ananias obeyed God and went to pray for Saul. The moment Ananias met him, he laid his hands on Saul and said, *"Brother Saul, the Lord, even Jesus, that appeared unto thee in the way as thou camest, hath sent me, that thou mightest receive thy sight, and be filled with the Holy Ghost"* (Acts 9:17).

Even the apostles didn't want to associate with Saul. They were not convinced of his conversion. As far as they knew, he had been on his way to Jerusalem to kill them, for they had seen no evidence to support that theory!

It took Barnabas to change their attitude. He brought Saul before them and explained *"how he had seen the Lord in the way, and that he had spoken to him, and how he had preached boldly at Damascus in the name of Jesus"* (Acts 9:27).

When the apostles saw the transformation that had taken place in Saul, they were amazed. He had turned one of the cruelest persecutors of the church into one of its champions. This man who had once been a threat to their own personal safety and to the message they preached now went about proclaiming *"Christ in the synagogues, that he is the Son of God"* (Acts 9:20).

If the Holy Spirit could transform Saul into Paul, totally reorchestrating his life and the purpose for his very existence, imagine how He could transform you and me. Just one touch of His presence can change the course of our lives so that we will walk in His ways to accomplish His marvelous will and not our own.

Acts 10: He will change your tradition.

My hometown of Jaffa, Israel, had the ancient Greek name of Joppa in Bible times. As a boy I climbed to the Citadel, a lighthouse on the highest spot overlooking the harbor. Near this lighthouse is the house of Simon the Tanner, where the apostle Peter had an experience that changed the world.

On the roof of Simon's house, Peter had a vision of God lowering four-footed animals, reptiles, and birds in a giant sheet. God told Peter to kill and eat them. Peter, a man bound by tradition, said, *"Not so, Lord; for I have never eaten any thing that is common or unclean"* (Acts 10:14).

The Lord answered, *"What God hath cleansed, that call not thou common"* (Acts 10:15).

While Peter thought about the vision, the Holy Spirit told him to go downstairs and meet three men who were looking for him. Furthermore, God said he should *"go with them, doubting nothing: for I have sent them"* (Acts 10:20).

Peter despised Gentiles. He was so bound by his Jewishness that, before this moment, he would not even talk to them. But because of the vision he had seen, Peter discarded his tradition and went on to have a great ministry to the Gentile world.

Only the Holy Spirit can produce such a radical transformation. What kind of transformation do you need? Ask Him to do it.

Acts 11: He will change your outlook.

At times the Holy Spirit will reveal the future in preparation for trials and struggles coming your way. We find one instance of that in Acts 11:28: *"And there stood up one of them*

69

named Agabus, and signified by the spirit that there should be great dearth throughout all the world: which came to pass in the day of Claudius Caesar."

When this kind of revelation occurs, there is no natural explanation for it. However, there is an inner knowing that what has been revealed to your heart will take place and that because of God's grace, He is preparing you for it. Through prayer you can be prepared for what is ahead. I challenge you this day to commit to a deeper, more intimate prayer life than you've ever known.

Acts 12: He'll change your prayer life.

It would have been totally impossible for me to develop a prayer life without first becoming acquainted with the Holy Spirit. It flows so naturally when you know Him, yet apart from Him it is impossible.

When the believers heard that Peter was in prison, *"prayer was made without ceasing of the church unto God for him"* (Acts 12:5). They learned what it meant to pray without ceasing.

This continual prayer was offered until the answer came for Peter and he was delivered from Herod's prison by an angel. The chains fell off and he walked out of the prison (see Acts 12:7).

In fact, God's divine intervention on Peter's behalf was so miraculous and out of the ordinary that Peter wasn't even sure it was actually happening. He thought he was having a vision. Just moments before his liberation, Peter had been sleeping, chained between two soldiers. Suddenly a bright light appeared in the prison, and an angel of the Lord woke him and said, *"Arise up quickly"* (Acts 12:7). And with that, Peter's chains fell off! Then the angel of the Lord told him to put his sandals on, wrap his garment around him, and follow him. Not until he was outside the prison, walking on the streets, did Peter realize what had really happened!

The believers in the book of Acts were able to pray without ceasing for Peter because of the presence of the Holy Spirit, for prayer without ceasing is impossible without the help and assistance of the Holy Spirit. Ask Him today to develop that in you and He will. Psalm 80:18 declares, *"Quicken us, and we will call upon thy name."* Ask Him to quicken and revive you daily and He will do it.

Acts 13: He will make your calling sure.

Since the moment the Holy Spirit called me to preach His Word, I have never had one moment of doubt concerning my calling. It was not an occupation chosen by trial and error, nor was it a decision I made for myself. God directed and I said yes.

Throughout the book of Acts you will meet people who were called by God for a specific task. During a service at a church at Antioch, the Holy Spirit said, *"Separate me Barnabas and Saul for the work whereunto I have called them"* (Acts 13:2).

The church fasted, prayed, and laid their hands on them before sending the evangelists away. Scripture tells us they were *"sent forth by the Holy Ghost"* to the island of Cyprus (Acts 13:4).

There is only one way to know God's direction and leadership for your life. Continue to seek Him until He makes your calling sure—and remember, the Holy Spirit speaks through the Scriptures and through godly people, as well as directly to your heart.

Acts 14: He will change your authority.

As Paul and Barnabas ministered from city to city, there was

71

a power in their preaching, an authority and confirmation to their words and deeds.

When they came to Lystra, a man who had never walked, heard them. And as Paul spoke, the man's faith came alive and Paul, *"perceiving that he had faith to be healed, Said with a loud voice, Stand upright on thy feet"* (Acts 14:9-10). And the man—crippled from birth—leaped to his feet and began to walk.

Paul was watching the man while he preached, but waited to speak until the man was ready for his miracle. The Holy Spirit gave Paul that perception to know when the time for the miracle was right. Then, He gave Paul the authority to minister miraculously to that man. Allow the Holy Spirit to increase your authority, too.

72
Acts 15: He will be your partner in decision making.

I have discovered that one of the greatest benefits of walking with the Holy Spirit is that I don't have to make decisions alone. I have a Teacher, a Guide, and a Counselor to help me every step of the way. He is more than an advisor. He is deeply interested in everything that concerns you, and He wants to be a partner in settling every issue in your life.

When the church at Jerusalem sent a letter to the Gentile believers at Antioch, they wrote something of profound importance. They said, *"It seemed good to the Holy Ghost, and to us"* (Acts 15:28). They didn't make decisions on their own. These wise people knew to let the Holy Spirit help them.

The Spirit of God is a wonderful Companion, but He wants to become more than that to you. He knows the end from the beginning in everything you face. Allow Him to participate in your decision making. You could not find a better Helper!

Acts 16: He will change your direction.

More than once our staff has made detailed plans for a major crusade when the Holy Spirit has clearly warned me, "Don't go." I can't explain it and I certainly don't understand it, but I know how much He cares for me, and I have to obey His leading. When He speaks that way, we change our plans.

When Paul and Silas traveled through the region of Galatia, they *"were forbidden of the Holy Ghost to preach the word in Asia, After they had come to Mysia, they assayed to go into Bithynia, but the Spirit suffered them not"* (Acts 16:6-7).

That is when the Holy Spirit gave Paul a vision of a man from Macedonia, pleading, *"Come over into Macedonia, and help us"* (Acts 16:9).

You've heard this before, but it won't hurt to be reminded: "When God closes one door, He always opens another." It's true. Opening and closing doors is one way He clearly directs us.

When you let God chart your course, you will be on the right path. Remember, the Holy Spirit never makes a mistake. Trust Him to lead, and He will do so with perfection.

Acts 17: He will change your world.

At Thessalonica, Paul and Silas were involved in a near riot, but it really wasn't their fault. The Jews were so jealous of the crowds who were listening to Paul explain the Scriptures that they rounded up some unsavory characters at the marketplace, formed a mob, and started a riot in the city (see Acts 17:1-5).

73

The throng shouted to the rulers of the city, *"These that have turned the world upside down are come hither also"* (Acts 17:6).

Their reputation preceded Paul and Silas, and news of their activities spread quickly. Almost everywhere they went, they saw revival. People were turning to Christ, healings were taking place, and the Spirit of God was at work.

And He wants to do the same through you today. He really wants to change your world.

Years ago, someone told me, "Benny, the quickest way to turn your world upside down is to turn yourself right-side up." It was good advice.

Acts 18: He will change your understanding.

You will begin to know the ways of God more perfectly. You will find that you now understand truths or things in God's Word that were once baffling to you. I feel fortunate to be surrounded in ministry by people who have a deep dedication to the task God has called them to do. I am grateful for the sensitivity and understanding with which they minister as they serve Him. They have developed such sensitivity and understanding as a result of their relationship with the Holy Spirit.

"And he began to speak boldly in the synagogue: whom when Aquila and Priscilla heard, they took him unto them, and expounded unto him the way of God more perfectly" (Acts 18:26).

Acts 19: He will change others as His presence comes upon you.

When Paul came to Ephesus, he found some disciples and said to them, *"Have ye received the Holy Ghost since ye believed?"* The disciples to whom he spoke answered, *"We have not so much as heard whether there be any Holy Ghost"* (Acts 19:2).

We find that Paul taught them about the Holy Spirit and then laid hands upon them, and *"the Holy Ghost came on them"* (Acts 19:6).

Later in this same chapter, we find that *"God wrought special miracles by the hands of Paul: So that even from his body were brought unto the sick handkerchiefs or aprons, and the diseases departed from them, and the evil spirits went out of them"* (Acts 19:11-12). The presence of God was so strong on Paul that the anointing could be transferred by the laying on of hands and upon handkerchiefs. The sick were healed and evil spirits were cast out because the anointing of the Holy Spirit lingered so powerfully upon Paul.

Paul was greatly opposed in Ephesus by both the Jewish establishment and the followers of pagan religions (see Acts 19:9, 23-41). Never forget that the greater the opposition, the greater the power. In this difficult and dangerous city, *"God wrought special [literally, "extraordinary"] miracles"* (Acts 19:11). The Holy Spirit wants to do the same today, only if we are willing to pay the price, which means being totally, completely, wholly yielded to Him.

Acts 20: He will change your leadership.

God did not send His Spirit to earth as our Helper so that we could neglect our duties. As a Counselor and Guide, He shows us how to take responsibility for God's work and empowers us to do it with supernatural results, giving us a place of responsibility and influence in the kingdom.

Paul's farewell message to the Ephesian elders after three years of ministry came straight from his heart. His objective was for them to accept the mantle of leadership in the church. He told them with great emotion, *"Take heed therefore unto yourselves, and to all the flock, over the which the Holy Ghost hath made you overseers, to feed the church of God, which he hath purchased with his own blood"* (Acts 20:28).

Paul issued this challenge with great confidence because he knew the Holy Spirit would give them all they needed to succeed, in spiritual leadership. He also knew that after his departure, *"grievous wolves [will] enter in among you, not sparing the flock"* (Acts 20:29). They would be determined to distort the truth and deceive the disciples.

God took Moses, who *"was very meek, above all the men which were upon the face of the earth"* (Numbers 12:3), and made him into a great leader. And He wants to do the same for you and through you today.

Acts 21: He will change your insight.

At times God has given me a specific word of prophecy for someone. Sometimes this will happen as an individual stands before me on the platform in the crusades. So far, however, the Lord has never asked of me what he asked of Agabus. When He gave Agabus a word from God for Paul— the Billy Graham of his day—he did not shrink from delivering it. At Caesarea, Agabus walked up to the apostle, took Paul's belt, and bound it around his own hands and feet. Then he said, *"Thus saith the Holy Ghost, So shall the Jews at Jerusalem bind the man that owneth this girdle, and shall deliver him into the hands of the Gentiles"* (Acts 21:11).

Only a man who had a mighty relationship with the Lord could make such a declaration.

Agabus's prophecy gave Paul insight into the difficult days ahead for him. He responded, *"What mean ye to weep and to break mine heart? for I am ready not to be bound only, but also to die at Jerusalem for the name of the Lord Jesus"* (Acts 21:13).

When we receive insight, it makes us bold and loyal, even unto death. When you know the Holy Spirit, you will see beyond the temporal, and not even death will frighten you.

Acts 22: He will change your commission.

Do you remember the moment you gave your heart to Christ? Paul's experience on the Damascus road was one he certainly could not forget. Like so many people, Paul was sincere—but sincerely wrong. Paul had no use for Jesus or His followers. Although he took his opposition of Christ to an extreme, he was not unlike many of us in the days before we met the Master.

And meet the Master he did! Paul gave his testimony of being blinded by a bright light, and how his night turned to day. He had seen the resurrected Christ, and that convinced him of the truth of the Gospel. From a changed recognition came a changed commission. *"The God of our fathers hath chosen thee, that thou shouldest know his will, and see that Just One, and shouldest hear the voice of his mouth. For thou shalt be his witness unto all men of what thou hast seen and heard"* (Acts 22:14-15).

Acts 23: He will increase your influence.

People continue to ask, "Does the Lord really speak to people?" My answer is an unqualified yes! I know this not only because of my personal experience, but because God's Word says it's true!

The city of Jerusalem was in such an uproar over Paul that the commander of the prison thought the mobs would take him away by force. In the midst of that crisis, Scripture says, *"The Lord stood by him, and said, Be of good cheer, Paul: for as thou hast testified of me in Jerusalem, so must thou bear witness also at Rome"* (Acts 23:11).

Because of God's power on his life, Paul was brought before Caesar and testified for the Master. And as Paul remained faithful, God opened doors supernaturally for him and brought him into a greater dimension of influence before men of power and authority for the glory of God. He became, and is to this day, a hero of our faith.

Acts 24: He will establish your eternal hope.

The apostle Paul was on a mission. No matter what his circumstances were, he presented the Gospel. And Paul was supernaturally aided to do what he did, and nothing could shake his commitment.

As Paul stood accused before the governor, he said, *"But this I confess unto thee, that after the way which they call heresy, so I worship the God of my fathers, believing all things which are written in the law and in the prophets: And have hope toward God, which they themselves also allow, that there shall be a resurrection of the dead, both of the just and the unjust"* (Acts 24:14-15). Here Paul declares that he was given hope—the marvelous hope given only by the Holy Spirit, even in the presence of his enemies.

Acts 25: He will change your level of confidence.

Paul's reliance on the Lord never wavered. In the face of the Jews who hated him and the Romans who were baffled by him, he remained not only confident, but lively and aggressive!

He boldly maintained that *"to the Jews have I done no*

wrong, as thou very well knowest . . . I appeal unto Caesar"
(Acts 25:10-11). Make no mistake, the Romans had heard
Paul's message—even though they didn't quite understand
it yet. In fact, the Roman official noted his understanding that
Paul's message was about "Jesus, which was dead, whom Paul
affirmed to be alive" (Acts 25:19). What baffled them was that
Paul not only affirmed it, he was totally convinced of it.

How did Paul know Christ was alive in the loneliness of
a prison cell, in the pain of a flogging, or in the desolation
of a shipwreck? Through his never-ending companionship
with the Holy Spirit he knew. The Lord Jesus not only
promised to send the Comforter, but He delivered on that
commitment. The Holy Spirit will be with you, too, in all
the tough times you encounter.

Acts 26: He will change your witness.

Before God healed my stuttering tongue, I would avoid
speaking if at all possible. Even as a young Christian, I would
never volunteer to read the Scripture in public or give even a
short testimony.

But what a change took place when God healed me as I
preached my first sermon in late 1974. My tongue was
loosed, and it seems I have not stopped talking since.

Paul took every opportunity to present his testimony,
too, and to bring deliverance to the captives. His defense
before King Agrippa was so strong it has been a model of
study for legal scholars. There was strength in his witness and
power in his words. When he was finished, Agrippa said,
"Almost thou persuadest me to be a Christian" (Acts 26:28).

Almost anyone can produce a speech, but only the
Spirit of God can produce a testimony.

Acts 27: He will change your chaos into peace.

On his final journey to Rome, Paul was a prisoner on a ship with 276 passengers. After two weeks of storm-tossed seas, the apostle was the only person who knew the meaning of peace. As day was about to dawn, *"Paul besought them all to take meat, saying, This day is the fourteenth day that ye have tarried and continued fasting, having taken nothing"* (Acts 27:33).

He not only urged them to eat for survival, but he reassured them, *"There shall not an hair fall from the head of any of you"* (Acts 27:34). In times of testing, only the peace from above can calm the storm.

I know what it is like to be near the point of death. In 1983, while flying with six passengers in a Cessna aircraft at 11,000 feet, we ran out of fuel near Avon Park, Florida. I was asleep, but not for long. "We're in trouble. Pray! Pray!" were the first words I heard from our pilot, Don.

Everyone began crying out in fear. But suddenly a great peace came over me. I said, "Don, it's going to be all right. No one will be killed!"

God used those words to calm the passengers. "Please don't cry," I told them. "Just relax. God isn't finished with me."

We crash-landed in a field and there were some injuries, but I did not have a scratch. Deep within my spirit I had the assurance, "It's going to be all right."

Over twelve years later, I faced similar circumstances in 1995. We were returning from a miracle crusade in Japan, heading for Hawaii where we were to land and refuel. With less than two hours left in our flight, silence in the cabin was interrupted by the pilot's voice as he said, "Pastor Benny, I think you'd better pray." He went on to explain that there was a problem with the instruments and we were lost somewhere over the Pacific.

I immediately began to pray, and even though some of those who were with me were fearful, a peace settled over me. Although the circumstances were impossible in the natural, I felt a supernatural assurance that everything was going to be all right.

The pilots continued to work with the instruments in the cockpit, but to no avail. With a rapidly diminishing fuel supply and in the midst of growing tension, the unexplainable confidence within me continued—everything was going to be fine.

Suddenly and miraculously, our pilots made contact with someone who suggested that they tune to a radio station and use it to help guide them toward land. They did just that and landed with less than an hour's fuel remaining. In fact, our pilots told us we were flying on fumes!

Although I always knew that our safe landing was a direct result of God's divine intervention, I never knew any of the details. Just recently at our Hawaii Miracle Crusade, however, I had the privilege of meeting one of the gentlemen who was working in the control tower that night. He explained that although he wasn't responsible for that particular airspace, he felt an urging by the Holy Spirit to get involved when he heard one of the other controllers attempting to contact a private plane that was overdue. He said landings are scheduled in advance, and the control tower was expecting our plane. However, because the plane was off course due to the instrumentation problem, we never showed up on their radar. As they attempted to contact us, they finally made radio contact with the plane but had no idea of our location.

As the man became more involved, he felt an over-whelming inner urging to pray. He explained, "I didn't know who was on that plane, but I knew that I had to help. When nothing else worked, someone in the tower suggested tuning into a radio station to help guide the plane in," the gentle-man said. "I instantly remembered a 50,000-watt Christian radio station on the island which I listened to often. I sug-gested that frequency, and immediately, your pilots tuned in to the signal. That's how my friend and I in the control tower helped get your plane down on the ground safely."

Then he added, "For seven years I have wondered who was on that airplane that night but had no way of finding out. Recently, I was talking to some friends at our church about the situation, and they told me they knew the other part of the story. They said they were Covenant Partners with Benny Hinn Ministries, and Benny Hinn and some of his team were the individuals on that plane that night."

After the man finished his story, I gave him a big hug and thanked him for recognizing the voice of the Holy Spirit and for responding in obedience. Then I added, "Thank you for saving my life! God wasn't done with me yet!"

I have seen the Holy Spirit turn chaos into peace many, many times. And I am a living testimony to His ability to do so. Won't you allow Him to touch the chaos in your life with His deep and abiding peace?

Acts 28: He will change your conflict into victory.

Paul was shipwrecked off the island of Malta, and every pas-senger reached land in safety. But as they were building a fire for warmth, a viper came out of the heat and fastened itself onto Paul's hand.

When the island natives saw the snake hanging from his hand, they said to each other, *"No doubt this man is a murderer, whom, though he hath escaped the sea, yet vengeance suffereth not to live"* (Acts 28:4).

Instead of screaming, "I'm going to die! Get me some medicine!" Paul simply shook the serpent off and sustained no ill effects.

The islanders expected him to die instantly. After a while, when they realized he was going to live, *"they changed their minds, and said that he was a god"* (Acts 28:6).

Only the Holy Spirit can turn your conflict into victory. He'll do it for you!

CHAPTER SEVEN

DEEPER
with the PRECIOUS
HOLY SPIRIT

As you move into a deeper relationship with the Holy Spirit, it is important to understand several principles about His anointing. Often I am asked, "How do you recognize the anointing? How do you know that the anointing is there in your services?"

God says in Ezekiel 11:19-20:

And I will give them one heart, and I will put a new spirit within you; and I will take the stony heart out of their flesh, and will give them an heart of flesh: That they may walk in my statutes, and keep mine ordinances, and do them: and they shall be my people, and I will be their God.

A stony heart is the only kind of heart that can never recognize the anointing. You cannot discern the Holy Spirit's presence if your heart is not tuned into His. And God Almighty must do a new work in you before you can discern His precious anointing.

The Gentle Holy Spirit

When I met the Holy Spirit I had no idea that He was as gentle as He truly is. From so many things I had been taught, I was almost afraid of the Holy Spirit. I had heard about blasphemy against the Holy Spirit and how that is unforgivable. And I had heard about the Spirit of God being grieved and how easily He is wounded. Others presented the Holy Spirit as a loud, uncontrollable personality.

What I discovered is that the Holy Spirit is a Gentleman. He is holy—so kind, precious, and beautiful. Jesus called Him the Comforter. The Bible calls Him the Spirit of holiness, the glorious Spirit, Spirit of grace, gracious Spirit. Someone who is gracious is not rude. The Bible calls Him many great names, as we have already discovered in previous chapters. If you really want to know what the Holy Ghost is like, study a dove.

I met the Holy Ghost on December 21 many years ago. When I met Him, I honestly didn't know what kind of relationship would develop. All these years later, and I am still getting to know Him. I feel as if I have just begun. And I keep discovering that the more I know Him, the more I see how little I know. And He continues to teach me, show me, and lead me step by step.

The Bible says that they who are led by the Spirit are the sons of God. Any person who is led by the Spirit must have a relationship with Him. The word for "led" in the Greek ties in fellowship. How can you be led by someone you don't even know?

Before I came into this fellowship, I attended a very nice Pentecostal church in Canada. I sat there as a young Christian, hungry for God. I had grown up attending a Catholic school, and my Greek Orthodox parents were very quiet people. I was simply very hungry for God.

It wasn't long before I went to a Kathryn Kuhlman service. I had never seen an individual operate under the anointing of the Holy Spirit like Kathryn. Kathryn prayed over and over and over in that service: "Lord, help me cooperate with You. If only I can work better with You." I thought, what is she talking about?

The service was so different from anything else I had ever experienced before. The place was packed, and many people were fighting for front seats. There we sat in this church on a cold morning in Pittsburgh, and miracles began happening.

To this day I still recall one lady's healing. She was sitting on the third row, and to my right a girl began to scream, "I can see! I can see! I can see!" That whole section of the church erupted with praise. Finally Kathryn said, "What's happening over there?" They escorted the lady up to the stage, and she was almost hysterical. I sat watching, crying. The service lasted four hours. I saw wheelchairs emptied, blind folks healed, arthritis suddenly gone from formerly pain-filled bodies. It felt like four seconds, not four hours. I began realizing that everything was so different because of the Holy Spirit's anointing that fell during the service.

The Anointing in My Ministry

I was already preaching and ministering, so after attending Kathryn's meetings several times, I thought to myself, I am going to welcome the Holy Ghost to my meetings. I used to have Monday night services in Toronto in a place called the Evangelistic Center.

Kathryn always liked quietness, so I thought I would try that. I said, "Not a sound should be made." But people wouldn't be quiet. They kept saying, "Hallelujah! Praise the Lord! Bless You, Jesus." I love those phrases, but I felt as if we should be quiet.

Finally I said, "Please, quiet! Quiet." It took forever to get people to do what I felt the Holy Spirit wanted, and finally the place got quiet. Then I said, "Every eye close."

Frankly, even as everyone got quite, with all eyes closed, I began to think, "Oh God, I hope this thing works." I didn't know what I was doing. I just knew that it had worked with Kathryn Kuhlman, and felt I should do it, too.

I thought that maybe I would hear or feel something. Nothing. I didn't feel a thing. I didn't hear a thing. I was increasingly nervous. My eyes were closed as the place got quieter and quieter. I knew that sometimes Kathryn would say, "Something is happening. Something is happening." Yet I knew I couldn't say that, for nothing seemed to be taking place.

What I didn't know were the things happening in people's lives. Finally, I heard a big crash, and I opened my eyes. Except for me, no one was standing. Everybody was on the floor—from the piano player to the people in the back row. The worship leader was crying. I stood there looking at everything, knowing that this was the work of the Holy Spirit, and certainly nothing that I had caused.

I truly began learning the ways of the Spirit that day. God often uses the most unlikely places and times to teach you how to move in the anointing as you grow deeper in Him.

Ask the Holy Ghost to Be Your Teacher

After you become acquainted with the Holy Ghost by fellow-shipping with Him, you will understand that He longs for fellowship. Talk to Him. Spend time in prayer each and every day. You may ask, what if I talk and no one answers? Don't let that stop you. Talk to Him anyway. In fact, you quickly learn that the Holy Ghost often answers differently than you expect Him to. He is God. He is not restricted by human limitations. It is up to you to ask for spiritual discernment and guidance.

Don't utter a word before you say, "Holy Spirit, help me pray." Then you can open your Bible and ask Him, "Holy Spirit, please be my Teacher." That's exactly what I do all the time. Especially when the book *Good Morning, Holy Spirit* was published, people looked upon my relationship with Him as revolutionary. I believe the relationship with Him— mine or yours—simply means becoming acquainted with Him, continually learning from Him, and growing into an ever-deepening relationship.

It will transform your life when you realize you can talk with the Holy Spirit all during the day and night. Nothing happens without Him. He is included in everything. It seems totally normal to me. Though it is in the realm of the supernatural, it has become quite natural. Before I walk out to minister I say, "Holy Spirit, please walk out with me." Before I teach God's Word I say, "Holy Spirit, You be the Teacher. All I can do is talk, but You can teach." I have continual conversation with Him.

Sensitivity to the Holy Spirit

You can only become sensitive to someone after you are acquainted with him or her. The same is true with the Holy Spirit. Would you like to become so close to the Holy Ghost that when He moves, you move? That will happen as you spend time in prayer. Prayer gets you acquainted with Him. As you ask for His guidance, teaching, and help, He will respond in ways different from what you would expect.

He speaks to you through the Word as He teaches you. Sometimes He speaks to you directly—you receive an inner knowing. Other times He will send someone to speak in your life. The Holy Ghost is the Spirit of variety. He will never speak to you just one way. And as that happens, you learn to become sensitive to Him. I have prayed for years, "Lord, make me sensitive to You." When you pray that prayer, please understand that He will affect every area of your life. You will have to be more pliable than ever. God's will becomes an everyday walk. You learn to surrender very quickly rather than risk missing anything with Him.

Granted, some people are more sensitive to others by nature. Whether you are or not, it is vital to ask God to grant you the eternity-changing gift of sensitivity to the Holy Spirit. I pray for this all the time. I never want to become callous to Him, which human nature tends toward. The Lord has brought me to the place now where the ground of my heart is soft. Seeds can be planted deeply in soil that is soft, but if the ground is hard, the seed will not take deep root. The deeper you allow the Holy Spirit to enter your heart, the deeper will be your walk with Him and the more powerful His anointing on you.

The Price of a Deeper Relationship

To walk with the Holy Ghost, you must be willing to pay the price. What is that price? You must be willing to walk away from things of the world that would separate you from the Lord.

Remember, the Lord will not reveal Himself to an individual who is always in a hurry. Nor will He reveal Himself to an individual who places a time limit on Him. His fellowship is not cheap. Jesus went to the cross of Calvary that we might be able to become God's redeemed children. A great price was paid for you that you might have fellowship with Him. Going deeper with the Holy Spirit costs even more.

Many try to enter into His presence by saying, "I have ten minutes and that is all." Paying the price means giving your whole self, including your valuable time, to Him. We must rid ourselves of all other things that are on our minds when we seek to enter into His presence. God is not look-ing for a people who rush in and rush out, as if punching a spiritual time clock. He is looking to anoint those individu-als who are sensitive to Him and to His desire for unham-pered fellowship.

If you worship Him, He will honor you with His pres-ence. Worship invites His presence. This means learning to follow His leading and cooperating with Him, not trying to get Him to follow you. And as you learn to seek His pres-ence, miracles happen. Healing takes place. Lives are restored. Blessings flow.

Just remember, the Lord responds to hunger. Matthew 5:6 declares, *"Blessed are they which do hunger and thirst after righteousness: for they shall be filled."* The Lord fills the indi-vidual who is hungry for more of His presence. One sign of hungry people is that they respond to the anointing. They become like a sponge, soaking up every bit of God's pres-ence that they can. They understand that His presence is what makes them whole. A trickle leads to a gush then flows into a river of glory.

Have you ever seen a hungry baby at his mother's breast? That baby is very hungry in the beginning and eats quickly, but then after a while the baby quits sucking. When the baby realizes he wants more, he sucks again, just once or twice. Hunger for the Lord's presence is very much the same. When you start to feel empty, tell him again, "I need you, Lord." Ask him, "Fill me please, Lord."

A woman who lived in seventeenth-century France, Madam Jeanne Guyon, wrote about such truths in her book *Experiencing the Depths of Jesus Christ*. She said, "If you are starving and can find nothing to satisfy your hunger, then come. Come, and you will be filled." Religious leaders of the day persecuted her for the exact same thing I am sharing with you now. She said, "First, come before the Lord and begin to read. Stop reading just as soon as you feel yourself being drawn inwardly. Now, simply remain in stillness. By following your spirit, every encounter you have with the Lord is one that is perfect . . . no matter what the encounter is like." One word in prayer during moments like these can take you higher than hours of nonstop talking.

Anything you say that touches the Lord, He will respond and touch you back. Prayer does not have to be lifeless and dull. As you cooperate with and follow the Holy Spirit, your life will become the most wonderful experience every day.

How will His presence affect your life? You will have peace, no matter what circumstances come your way.

Ask for the Lord's Help

You can lift your hands right now and tell Him you are hungry for His presence and anointing. Ask Him to help you recognize His leading. Tell Him that you want to know the ways of the Spirit.

As you surrender yourself to the Lord, He will flow through you, bringing a fresh anointing to your life, a heart that is sensitive to the wind of the Spirit and a clean heart based on close fellowship with Him.

God will give you incredible assurance as you spend time with Him. In other words, faith will be stirred and will come alive inside of you. When that happens, you no longer merely hope that your prayers will be answered. You will know with surety that your heart's desires are being answered. But that first begins with a willing heart—pliable and open before Him.

$\mathscr{A}$ MIGHTY RUSHING WIND

The New Testament is filled with accounts of people who chose to go deeper with the Holy Spirit. I believe with all of my heart that same anointing is available to God's people.

Acts 2:1-2 declares, *"And when the day of Pentecost was fully come, they were all with one accord in one place. And suddenly there came a sound from heaven as of a rushing mighty wind, and it filled all the house where they were sitting."* The sound of a mighty rushing wind filled the whole house. You are God's house, the temple of the Holy Spirit, and that wind is about to come upon you, your home, and your family—filling you completely.

A new anointing of God will come into your life as you go deeper in your relationship with Him:

> The wilderness and the solitary place shall be glad for them; and the desert shall rejoice, and blossom as the rose. It shall blossom abundantly, and rejoice even with joy and singing: the glory of Lebanon shall be given unto it, the excellency of Carmel and Sharon, they shall see the glory of the LORD, and the excellency of our God. (Isaiah 35:1-2)

This prophecy is remarkable because it says the wilderness will be like a rose. The place that has been an unsettled, remote, and barren land to you is about to burst forth with life and beauty. A wasteland will become fragrant, colorful, and full of the splendor and glory of the Lord.

Growing up in Jaffa, Israel, every spring we would smell the beautiful fragrance of the cedar trees as the north winds blew south into Israel. When I woke up in the morning, I could smell the aroma of the cedars of Lebanon carried in by the wind.

Whenever you read about the glory of Lebanon in the Word of God, it deals with Lebanon's cedar trees. God says in His Word that the glory of Lebanon shall be given to the wilderness and a dry place. That means that the dry place in your life where there is no living water and no presence of God is about to experience a new atmosphere and recovered life.

Many dear Christians experience a beautiful presence of the Lord when they first give their lives to Him. The salvation experience and presence of the Holy Spirit are so cleansing, refreshing, and restoring that as trials and life's disappointments set in, believers often wish they could have the same beautiful presence they had when they were first filled with the Holy Spirit.

God's Word says that before the glory of God comes upon you, you are going to experience the glory of Lebanon. That means a new atmosphere even greater than anything you have ever experienced before is about to come upon your life.

There is a great move of God coming to the earth, but I believe that before this move of God comes upon your life, you are going to have to grow deeper in your relationship with Him. As God brings that new presence and His Holy

Spirit upon your life, it will strengthen you. You will become so strong in the Lord that you will want to go and tell others what God can do for them. Isaiah 35:3-4 says, *"Strengthen ye the weak hands, and confirm the feeble knees. Say to them that are of a fearful heart, be strong, fear not."*

After that, the next thing that will happen is the miraculous: *"Then the eyes of the blind shall be opened, and the ears of the deaf shall be unstopped. Then shall the lame man leap as an hart, and the tongue of the dumb sing: for in the wilderness shall waters break out, and streams in the desert"* (Isaiah 35:5-6).

Even the enemies that have inhabited the dry ground in your life shall be removed. In their place, there will be deliverance and springs of living water bursting forth. Isaiah 35:7 says, *"And the parched ground shall become a pool, and the thirsty land springs of water: in the habitation of dragons, where each lay, shall be grass with reeds and rushes."* Dragons speak of demonic powers that have tried to influence you, harm you, and keep you pressed down. The waters of the Holy Ghost will move those dragons out of your way.

Finally, a righteous and holy life will be yours:

> *And an highway shall be there, and a way, and it shall be called The way of holiness; the unclean shall not pass over it; but it shall be for those: the wayfaring men, though fools, shall not err therein. No lion shall be there, nor any ravenous beast shall go up thereon, it shall not be found there; but the redeemed shall walk there: And the ransomed of the LORD shall return, and come to Zion with songs and everlasting joy upon their heads: they shall obtain joy and gladness, and sorrow and sighing shall flee away.* (Isaiah 35:8-10)

As you go deeper with the Holy Spirit, God can remove even the sorrow and sighing from your life, and He will replace it with joy and gladness.

Seven Results of the Wind of the Spirit

The wind of God is the atmosphere of the Spirit, and every time that the wind of God appeared in the Bible a number of things happened. Acts 2:3-4 says that after the mighty rushing wind came that *"there appeared unto them cloven tongues like as of fire, and it sat upon each of them. And they were all filled with the Holy Ghost."*

- **The wind of the Spirit removes judgment.** Genesis 8:1 says, *"And God remembered Noah, and every living thing, and all the cattle that was with him in the ark: and God made a wind to pass over the earth, and the waters asswaged."* When the wind came after the flood, judgment ceased and blessings came. A new atmosphere always removes judgment.

- **The wind brings a new atmosphere into your life.** In Exodus 10:19, the wind removed locusts from the land: *"And the LORD turned a mighty strong west wind, which took away the locusts, and cast them into the Red sea; there remained not one locust in all the coasts of Egypt."* Locusts are symbolic of demonic powers. When a new atmosphere of the Spirit comes upon you, all demonic influence will leave your life.

- **The wind of the Spirit cleanses you.** Job 37:21 says, *"The wind passeth, and cleanseth them."* When God cleanses your life, you are free from anything that weighs you down as well as the sin that besets you so that you can *"run the race with patience that God has set before you"* (Hebrews 12:1).

98

- **The wind of the Spirit removes the chaff, or the things that hinder you.** Psalm 104:7 says, *"At thy rebuke they fled; at the voice of thy thunder they hasted away."* The wicked that have wrongfully affected your life and hindered you will leave when a new atmosphere of heaven comes upon your life. The presence of God brings the flesh into submission so that you can receive from heaven. The wind of the Spirit comes from the Word of the living God, from His very own lips. God is about to bring a new dimension of His presence upon you, so get ready by keeping yourself close to the Lord in prayer.

- **The wind of the Spirit brings fire from heaven.** Exodus 19:18 says, *"And mount Sinai was altogether on a smoke, because the LORD descended upon it in fire: and the smoke thereof ascended as the smoke of a furnace, and the whole mount quaked greatly."* In Isaiah, the Holy Ghost was the Spirit of fire that came upon Zion. Why fire? Because fire destroys sin: *"Then flew one of the seraphims unto me, having a live coal in his hand, which he had taken with the tongs from off the altar: And he laid it upon my mouth, and said, Lo, this hath touched thy lips; and thine iniquity is taken away, and thy sin purged"* (Isaiah 6:6-7). The fire of God is His power, and when it touches you it will cleanse you.

- **The wind of the Spirit destroys wickedness.** Isaiah 5:24 says, *"Therefore as the fire devoureth the stubble, and the flame consumeth the chaff, so their root shall be as rottenness, and their blossom shall go up as dust: because they have cast away the law of the LORD of hosts, and despised the word of the Holy One of Israel."* The wind of the Spirit will destroy every bit of evil, incorrigible sin, and immorality surrounding you; you will no longer be affected by the enemy's vice.

- **The wind of the Spirit brings the protection of God upon your life.** Isaiah 4:5 says, *"And the LORD will create upon every dwelling place of mount Zion, and upon her assemblies, a cloud and smoke by day, and the shining of a flaming fire by night: for upon all the glory shall be a defence."* The anointing itself is a combination of wind and fire, and it will protect you from demonic powers.

Where the Spirit of the Lord is, there is liberty. There is no return to bondage in Christ Jesus. Once you receive liberty, you are free: *"If the Son therefore shall make you free, ye shall be free indeed"* (John 8:36). The wind of the Holy Spirit brings such freedom and joy into your life!

Amazing Grace

We do not deserve God's blessings, and that is why we receive them by grace. God's goodness, provision, and blessings are freely given to you today. Ephesians 2:8 says, *"For by grace are ye saved through faith; and that not of yourselves: it is the gift of God."*

Consider this story as you reflect upon God's grace toward you: Suppose a man had been waiting to have a son of his own for a long time. Then finally he became a daddy. He loved his little boy, and took him everywhere. The father gave his son all he had, because his love was so great for him. But everything suddenly changed one day. A man showed up and killed the boy. The daddy who'd waited so long to have this child found his boy dead.

The father of the child would have three choices of what he could do next: First, he could go and kill the man who'd killed his son, or take revenge, and for that he would go to prison. Second, he could let the law of the land take care of the man who'd killed his son, or allow justice to take its course. Third, he could forgive the murderer, adopt the murderer as his own son, and then give that murderer all that belonged to his boy, giving the man amazing grace.

Amazing grace is what God, the Father did for you and me. Humanity put His Son on the cross, but He did not kill us, nor did He send us to the courts. He said, "I forgive you, I adopt you, and I give you everything that belongs to My Son."

In the natural, it is impossible to have that kind of grace—it's hard to even try to comprehend it—but God had it. If God loves you that much, you must understand that He wants you to recover all. The Lord wants you to have His anointing, His power, and every single promise in the Word. God does not want you to experience lack or loss in any area of your life, and He stands waiting to move on your behalf today as you call upon the name of Jesus.

Where Are You Digging?

All of these mighty promises are yours, yet you must first learn where and how to find God's blessing. Can you picture a man digging a well where there is no water? Just as you imagine, he would be toiling and wasting his energy, essentially working for nothing. Yet so many Christians toil and never find the water they have been digging for. *"For my people have committed two evils; they have forsaken me the fountain of living waters, and hewed them out cisterns, broken cisterns, that can hold no water"* (Jeremiah 2:13).

There are two very important points in this scripture:

they forsook the fountain of all living waters, and they had broken cisterns that held no water. Neither is acceptable. We must not become dried-up Christians lacking water, life, and the knowledge and love of God. How do you prevent your life from becoming dry? Begin to lift your hands and ask the Holy Spirit to lead you to the water.

A powerful portion of God's Word that will help keep you and me drawing living water is contained in 1 Kings 19:11-13:

> *And he said, Go forth, and stand upon the mount before the LORD. And, behold, the LORD passed by, and a great and strong wind rent the mountains, and brake in pieces the rocks before the LORD; but the LORD was not in the wind: and after the wind an earthquake; but the LORD was not in the earthquake: And after the earthquake a fire; but the LORD was not in the fire: and after the fire a still small voice And it was so, when Elijah heard it, that he wrapped his face in his mantle, and went out, and stood in the entering in of the cave. And, behold, there came a voice unto him, and said, What doest thou here, Elijah?*

Why did Elijah wrap his face in his mantle? He did it to eliminate outside distraction and interference. At first he didn't hear God, but after he wrapped his face he began to hear. If we, like Elijah, can learn to focus on the Lord, allowing the cares of this world to fall aside, we, too, will hear God's voice.

Like Elijah, there is the wind and there is the earthquake and there is a fire. All of these led Elijah to the cave. God wasn't in the cave; he was just outside that cave. When the still, small voice came, Elijah went outside the cave and stood. The Lord asked, "What are you doing here?" The moment Elijah the prophet heard the voice of God, the Lord told him to go back to work (verse 15).

God's voice is not for our personal picnic. It is for service. There is a reason for it when God speaks. If you do as God shows you to do, His anointing will intensify upon you.

Recognizing God's Voice

Augustine said that for years and years he looked for God to come from heaven to him then realized He was already inside him all the time. We must never look for God to come from heaven and touch us. He is already within you.

Elijah understood this, and that is the reason he wrapped his mantle around his face. He was drawing within. How can you do as Elijah did? Through worship and stillness with God. Zechariah 2:13 declares, *"Be silent, O all flesh, before the LORD: for he is raised up out of his holy habitation."*

As you hold your peace, distractions begin to die and your heart will bubble up like a brook with fresh and living water.

Prayer enables you to begin knowing God's voice. When you pray, it moves God to move through you to touch people's lives. As you connect with His will, He'll flow out of you. When that happens, you may begin praying for the salvation of someone you haven't even seen for three years. All your plans go out the window, and instead of praying what you had planned to pray, you begin following the Holy Spirit and praying prayers that He leads you to pray. When this begins happening, you are open to the voice of the Spirit.

103

The Spirit of Prayer

As a child of God, you can go to the Holy Spirit and say, "I don't know what to pray, Holy Spirit. You are the Spirit of prayer. Help me pray." And He will help you. As prayers like this flood your being, you'll begin to cry out in repentance and thankfulness of the blood of Jesus that was shed for you. You begin to understand that God's voice does not come cheaply. A fresh revelation in His presence is not just for a thrill.

The Holy Spirit will lift your prayer as you pray it. When you sense that happening, keep praying that prayer until you feel it being lifted no more. Then wait before you move on to another prayer. The Holy Spirit will show you what to pray. As you do this, your prayers become directed by the Holy Spirit, rich and pleasing to God. Whether you are claiming a promise from His Word or are moved to believe for the salvation or healing of a loved one, welcome the Holy Spirit to pray through you. He is the one who energizes your prayer with life. But He can only do it if you give Him your vessel.

Times of Refreshing

In these moments, times of refreshing begin, times when praises and worship flow from your spirit that couldn't have flowed so freely before. A deep atmosphere of worship will begin to settle on you, causing you to say words like: "Jesus, You are glorious. Holy, holy, holy are You, Lord. You are worthy of my blessing. Jesus, I love You. There's none like You. You're altogether lovely. O, Holy Spirit, incline my heart toward God; remove the scales from my eyes that I might see His beauty. Take my dull ears and cause them to hear spiritual things. I can't do it on my own. Please help me win this battle over my flesh. Holy Spirit, bring me closer to my Lord."

In these moments, time of rest comes and you find the water. So quit digging wells where Jesus isn't standing. Find Him, and you'll find the water. The Scripture states: *"He that believeth on me, as the scripture hath said, out of his belly shall flow rivers of living water"* (John 7:38). The Holy Spirit will lead you to this place of blessing, plenty, and immeasurable love.

Do you realize that the Lord Jesus loves you more than He loves Himself? He died in your place. He gave Himself as a sacrifice for you. If He loved you less than He loved Himself, He would have said, "You die rather than Me." His love for you is a love so deep that words are inadequate to describe it. We simply cannot begin to fathom the depth of His love.

A River of Healing Water

I have experienced on different occasions in my life the wind of the Spirit and meetings where a mighty river of healing water appeared. I can vividly remember how I used to walk into Kathryn Kulhman's meetings and feel that atmosphere, and everything about me would change within minutes.

As you flourish in the house of the Lord, you will experience a healing river. The Word of God describes how the river washes over your entire being:

> And he brought me through the waters; the waters were
> to the ancles. Again he measured a thousand, and
> brought me through the waters; the waters were to the

knees. Again he measured a thousand, and brought me through; the waters were to the loins. Afterward he measured a thousand; and it was a river that I could not pass over: for the waters were risen, waters to swim in, a river that could not be passed over. (Ezekiel 47:3-5)

This passage of Scripture describes a river of healing. Everything that the river touches is healed. Ezekiel goes on to say, *"And it shall come to pass, that every thing that liveth, which moveth, whithersoever the rivers shall come, shall live: and there shall be a very great multitude of fish, because these waters shall come thither: for they shall be healed; and every thing shall live whither the river cometh"* (verse 9).

The Lord wants to bring you into recovery that washes over you and brings total restoration to your life. In the Lord you can rest; His peace and loving care surround. Psalm 23:2-3 says, *"He maketh me to lie down in green pastures: he leadeth me beside the still waters. He restoreth my soul."*

In John Bunyan's classic book *The Pilgrim's Progress,* Christian and his companion, Hope, rested by the river of God, or the river of the water of life. Of his dream Bunyan said:

On either side of the river was also a meadow, curiously beautified with lilies, and it was green all the year long. In this meadow they lay down and slept, for there they might lie down safely. When they awoke, they gathered again of the fruity of the trees, and drank again of the water of the river, and then lay down again to sleep.[1]

"Lord," you may ask, "How do I get into this river? I do not want just my feet wet. I want to be saturated in Your grace to the point where I am swimming in it. I want Your river of life to carry me."

"Come unto Me"

How do you get into the river that Ezekiel described? John 7:37-38 says this: *"In the last day, that great day of the feast, Jesus stood and cried, saying, If any man thirst, let him come unto me, and drink. He that believeth on me, as the scripture hath said, out of his belly shall flow rivers of living water."*

Jesus is the key. In John, Jesus said, *"I am the way, the truth, and the life: no man cometh unto the Father, but by me"* (John 14:6). He also said, *"If any man thirst, let him come unto me, and drink"* (John 7:37). He said that, for coming to Him, He would fill you so deeply that rivers will flow from your life and touch the world.

When you lay aside greed and selfish reasons and enter into fellowship with the Lord just because you love Him, a new atmosphere, fire, and anointing will come upon you. The Lord will fill you and then flow through you.

Jesus not only said you will be in the river, He also said that the river would be in you. From your innermost being shall flow rivers—not dead waters, but living and healing waters. The key is to come to Jesus and say, "Lord I am not here for what You can give me. I am here because I want You. I am not here for any other reason than to seek You."

I can tell you from experience that there is no want in your heart when Jesus is your everything. Psalm 23:1 says, *"The LORD is my shepherd; I shall not want."*

A shepherd is one who caringly tends to his flock and

107

provides all that they need. As you commit your whole self to the Lord, you will never want a thing. Psalm 34:10 says, *"They that seek the* LORD *shall not want any good thing."* In her book *Union with God,* Madam Guyon wrote:

> Thou, Lord, alone art all thy children need,
> And there is none beside;
> From thee the streams of blessedness proceed;
> In thee the bless'd abide.
> Fountain of life, and all-abounding grace,
> Our source, our center, and our dwelling place.[2]

What Keeps You from God's Presence?

Coming to Jesus is so simple, so powerful, and so life changing, yet believers are often kept from a deeper relationship with the Holy Spirit by distractions and the daily cares of this life. Nevertheless, we must daily persist in seeking the Lord's presence, because healing, restoration, and total recovery are found in Him.

A. W. Tozer, called a twentieth-century prophet, had a great impact on the body of Christ. He said:

> If we would progress spiritually, we must separate ourselves unto the things of God and concentrate upon them to the exclusion of a thousand things the worldly man considers important. We must cultivate God in the solitudes and silence; we must make the kingdom of God the sphere of our activity and labor in it like a farmer in his field, like a miner in the earth.[3]

The prophets longed for and never saw what we have in Christ Jesus, yet today so many Christians pass right by this deepening relationship. Moses came to the Lord and said, *"I beseech thee, shew me thy glory"* (Exodus 33:18). God answered Moses, *"Thou canst not see my face: for there shall no man see me, and live"* (33:20). The prophets longed to know God more and could not experience what you have in Christ today. We must not pass by the Lord and our very recovery, knowing that it is there but be too busy to pursue it.

The veil has been rent, and the way is open for you to boldly approach the throne of grace. The Lord said, *"Come unto me, all ye that labour and are heavy laden, and I will give you rest"* (Matthew 11:28). He also said, *"If any man thirst, let him come unto me, and drink"* (John 7:37).

Are you thirsty for the Lord's touch and presence in your life today? Jesus is the Source who can fill you. Like Ezekiel, you must go to the house of the Lord and drink. As you are filled with the Holy Spirit, God will be with you as He was with David on his journey to recover all.

109

Never Thirst Again

The infilling of the Holy Spirit is a daily process. We must come to Christ Jesus each day to be filled fresh again. Life's trials and situations will cause you to leak out what you have been filled with. Daily fellowship with the Lord is the key to abundant living. When you are thirsty, go to Jesus. He alone can fill you and satisfy your soul.

There is a river to go to where you will never thirst again. The psalmist said this:

> *O God, thou art my God; early will I seek thee: my soul thirsteth for thee, my flesh longeth for thee in a dry and thirsty land, where no water is; to see thy power and*

*thy glory, so as I have seen thee in the sanctuary.
Because thy lovingkindness is better than life, my lips
shall praise thee.* (Psalm 63:1-3)

The Word invites us to *"taste and see that the LORD is good:
blessed is the man that trusteth in him"* (Psalm 34:8). I have
good news for you; the more you taste, the hungrier you get.

Recently I was in prayer, and I heard God call my name
three times. He said, "Benny." I realized that the Lord was
trying to tell me something, and I spoke out just like
Samuel and said, "Yes, Lord." He said, "If you will search for
Me with all your heart you will find Me." I kneeled down
and got on my face before the Lord. I did not ask for a thing.
I simply said, "Jesus, come." That's all. "Just come."

In His presence, you will find all you will ever need. In
Christ Jesus, you are fully accepted, fully redeemed, and
fully forgiven. I love to sing the words to the song that say:

He is everything that my soul ever longed for.
He is everything that He promised, and so much
more.
He is more than amazing, more than miraculous,
more than marvelous,
That is what Jesus is to me.[4]

Who is Jesus to you? What mighty things has He done
for you? Have you told Him today that you long for His
presence more and more? The Holy Spirit longs for your fellowship today. Go, get on your knees in prayer, and wait on
the Lord. As you do, heaven's glory will fill your soul. He
longs to rush into your life like a mighty wind.

A FINAL NOTE

When Saul of Tarsus was blinded by the great light on the road to Damascus, a man by the name of Ananias was led by the Spirit to go to the house where Saul was staying. Here is what happened next: *"And Ananias went his way, and entered into the house; and putting his hands on him said, Brother Saul, the Lord, even Jesus, that appeared unto thee in the way as thou camest, hath sent me, that thou mightest receive thy sight, and be filled with the Holy Ghost"* (Acts 9:17). Saul became the apostle Paul, who not only helped start many of the New Testament churches but also—under the inspiration of the Holy Spirit—penned half of the New Testament. The history of mankind was impacted forever as the apostle's relationship grew deeper and deeper with the Holy Spirit.

Nothing can replace a personal relationship with the Holy Spirit. He works mightily in the lives of people attuned to Him. The Upper Room experience, no matter where it happens, is wonderful, but it is only the first step on the road of ever-increasing, always-deepening fellowship.

The Lord longs to fellowship with you. Allow Him now to change your hearing, your speech, your vision, your actions, and every part of your being. He will show you what He wants you to do as you seek Him.

Daniel said that those who *"know their God shall be strong, and carry out great exploits"* (Daniel 11:32). Today more than ever, the Lord wants to fill you to hasten the day that the world will be transformed from a place of desolation into a land of beauty (2 Peter 3:12-14), for *"the wilderness will rejoice and blossom"* (Isaiah 35:1, NIV). And that is just the beginning: *"Then the eyes of the blind shall be opened, and the ears of the deaf shall be unstopped. Then the lame shall leap like a deer, and the tongue of the dumb sing. For waters shall burst forth in the wilderness, and streams in the desert"* (Isaiah 35:5-6).

What a mighty visitation! And the Lord wants you to be part of it! When the fullness of God's anointing fills you, you will feel as the psalmist did when he declared, *"Let God arise, let his enemies be scattered"* (Psalm 68:1).

The transforming power of the Holy Spirit is beyond measure. And the benefits of His grace exceed our ability to describe. So much will happen when your deepening walk with the Holy Spirit transforms your life:

- **He will turn your wilderness into a fruitful place,** for *"the spirit [will] be poured upon us from on high, and the wilderness be a fruitful field, and the fruitful field be counted for a forest"* (Isaiah 32:15).
- **He will cause you to walk with God:** *"And I will put my spirit within you, and cause you to walk in my statutes, and ye shall keep my judgments, and do them"* (Ezekiel 36:27).
- **You will know God's presence:** *"Neither will I hide my face any more from them: for I have poured out my spirit . . . saith the Lord GOD"* (Ezekiel 39:29).
- **You will understand God's Word better:** *"Behold, I will pour out my spirit unto you, I will make known my words unto you"* (Proverbs 1:23).
- **You will become a new person,** for *"old things are passed away; behold, all things are become new"* (2 Corinthians 5:17).

- **He will give you rest:** *"For thus saith the Lord GOD . . . In returning and rest shall ye be saved; in quietness and in confidence shall be your strength: and ye would not"* (Isaiah 30:15).
- **He will bring excellence into your life,** as with Daniel: *"Then this Daniel was preferred above the presidents and princes, because an excellent spirit was in him; and the king thought to set him over the whole realm"* (Daniel 6:3).

The writer of Hebrews declares, *"How much more shall the blood of Christ, who through the eternal Spirit offered Himself without spot to God, cleanse your conscience from dead works to serve the living God?"* (Hebrews 9:14, NKJV). From dead works to service for the King! What could be better?

The Holy Spirit is eternal; He has always been, He is, and always will be. He is without beginning or end. He is the same, yesterday, today, and forever!

He is reliable and very loving. He never lets you down and is always understanding and so very patient. Truthfully, I've just begun to know him, and I know there is so much more to discover about Him.

Start now to seek a deeper relationship with the Holy Spirit. Grow in that relationship. Let Him change your life. Seek to know Him with your whole heart and to fellowship with Him. As you do, the glory of His presence will touch your life and help you to continue going deeper with the Holy Spirit.

My prayer for you is that your life will never be the same!

NOTES

Introduction

    1. R. A. Torrey, *Holy Spirit* (Lynnwood, WA: Emerald Books, 2002), 8.

    2. Torrey, *Holy Spirit,* 8.

Chapter 1: A Deeper Dimension

    1. William Barclay., *The Daily Study Bible* (Philadelphia: Westminster Press, 1958).

Chapter 2: The Holy Spirit

    1. Lewis Sperry Chafer, *Systematic Theology,* vol. 7 (Dallas: Dallas Seminary Press, 1948), 188.

Chapter 3: The Father and the Holy Spirit

    1. John F. Walvoord, *The Doctrine of the Holy Spirit,* as quoted in Chafer, *Systematic Theology,* 20.

Chapter 5: The Holy Spirit and You

    1. *Discipleship Journal,* no. 36, 11.

    2. Ibid., 7.

    3. Joseph Bayly, *Decision Magazine,* May 1978.

    4. Laird Harris, Gleason L. Archer, and Bruce K. Waltke, *Theological Wordbook of the Old Testament* (Chicago: Moody, 1980), vol. 1, 304.

    5. Ibid., 103.

    6. *The Autobiography of Bertrand Russell* (New York: Little, Brown, 1967).

    7. John F. Walvoord and Roy B. Zuck, eds., *Bible*

Knowledge Commentary, Old Testament (Wheaton, IL: Victor Books, 1985), 1056.

8. Don Meredith, *Who Says Get Married?* (Nashville: Thomas Nelson), 42.

9. *Single Adult Ministries Newsletter,* vol. 17, no. 5, March 1990, 1.

10. Robert Hanna, *A Grammatical Aid to the Greek New Testament* (Grand Rapids: Baker, 1983), 348.

11. Chafer, *Systematic Theology*, 188.

Chapter 6: The Work of the Holy Spirit

1. Dennis Bennett, *The Holy Spirit and You* (Plainfield, NJ: Logos International, 1971), 28.

Chapter 8: A Mighty Rushing Wind

1. John Bunyan, *The Pilgrim's Progress* (Chicago: Moody Press, 2002), 126-27.

2. Jeanne Guyon, *Union with God* (Jacksonville, FL: Seed Sowers, 1981), 80.

3. A.W. Tozer, *We Travel an Appointed Way* (Camp Hill, PA: Christian Publications, 1988), 26.

4. "More Than Wonderful." Words and music by Lanny Wolfe. Copyright © 1982 Lanny Wolfe Music. All rights controlled by Gaither Copyright Management. Used by permission.